822
W747
1972   Wilson   495   76
            Strindberg

                          c.1

D1442392

BOOKS BY COLIN WILSON:

The Outsider Cycle

The Outsider
Religion and the Rebel
The Stature of Man
The Strength to Dream
Origins of the Sexual Impulse
Beyond the Outsider

Introduction to the New Existentialism

Novels
Ritual in the Dark
The Philosopher's Stone
The Black Room

Autobiography
Voyage to a Beginning
The Occult

Strindberg

Strindberg

A PLAY IN TWO SCENES
by Colin Wilson

RANDOM HOUSE · NEW YORK

ISBN: 0-394-46554-7

Library of Congress Catalog Card Number: 70-159390

Manufactured in the United States of America by

The Haddon Craftsmen, Inc., Scranton, Pa.

2 4 6 8 9 7 5 3

FIRST PRINTING

FOR
ALFRED BURKE
who brought Strindberg to life

CHARACTERS

August Strindberg
Otto Steinmetz—*a Freudian psychologist*
The Judge
The Prosecutor
Dr. Gustav Böök—*a literary critic*

Siri von Essen—*Strindberg's first wife*
Harriet Bosse—*Strindberg's third wife*
Ina Forstén
Fanny Falkner

Part One

The scene is the room of Strindberg's flat in the Blue Tower, Drottninggatan 85, Stockholm. The room is in almost total darkness, the only light coming from the moon. It illuminates a bed in which there are two figures.

One of the figures in the bed begins to chuckle, softly at first; then the chuckle becomes a harsh laugh. The man gets out of bed and lights the gas. STRINDBERG is wearing blue silk pajamas. Sixty years old, he still looks much as he did in his youth: the mane of hair, with the sideboards well trimmed, the small mustache and the tiny crop of beard that sprouts under the middle of his lower lip, but does not cover his chin. The big head is leonine, the face a little haggard, the eyes tense and haunted—a man who never relaxes completely.

The room is seen to be small, with old-fashioned mahogany furniture. But the table is occupied with chemical apparatus: retorts and flasks and a large methylated spirit burner made from a round bottle. There is a telephone on a corner table, and STRINDBERG now goes to this. He winds a handle, and in a throaty, unnatural voice, asks:

STRINDBERG   Hello, hello . . . Can you give me two-seven-one? *(Then he sits sideways in the chair and stares*

across at the bed, muttering) Dreams and tears, dreams
and tears. *(Suddenly there is a faint sound from over-
head. He starts and puts the phone down, looking above
suspiciously. Then he tiptoes to the door, opens it, and
peers outside. He comes back muttering)* Whore. Nymphomaniac. *(He makes a strange flexing gesture with
his hands, stretching them and closing them, then clasps
them together. Looking at the ceiling again, he says
in a louder voice)* Whore! Bitch in heat! *(He goes over
to the bed cautiously, and pulls back the blanket slightly,
revealing a woman's head. A voice out of the telephone
can be heard saying: "Hello?"* STRINDBERG *takes hold
of the hair of the woman's head, and gives a tremendous
wrench. The head comes off, spilling some straw. It is
a dummy. He chuckles and looks at the ceiling. Then he
hears the voice from the telephone and rushes over to it)*

STRINDBERG Hello, Doctor Steinmetz? *(No reply; he
shouts)* Hello! Hello! *(A voice replies and he relaxes)*
Ah, thank God you're there, Steinmetz. I had to speak
to you . . . No, I had to put the telephone down. My wife
was knocking on the ceiling. Yes, my wife. In the room
above. She's up there now. I know it's her because it's
the children's nursery, and there's no one there at night
. . . Listen, I know it's late, but I had to tell you. *(His
voice becomes exultant)* It worked! Yes, your idea worked.
She came here five minutes ago and tried to seduce
me . . . Yes, I know it was her—I recognized the taste
of her tongue. Besides, it couldn't have been Frieda
or Siri. They wouldn't dare to try to take my pajamas off.
This one's a bitch in heat. She's like a madwoman. She

put her hand inside my pajama coat *(His own hand unconsciously does the same thing, caressing himself)* and started to undo the buttons. Then I started to kiss the dummy. *(He laughs)* Then she screamed and vanished. But she's back now. *(He looks at the ceiling)* She must want to find out who the woman is! She thinks it's Fanny . . . Yes, Fanny, the daughter of my landlady. Harriet thinks I'm having an affair with Fanny . . . Yes, all right. I'll come and see you in the morning. Not in the morning? When? Late afternoon. Five o'clock. All right, I'll do that . . . But what if Harriet comes back tonight? Shall I ring you? No? Why not? . . . Oh, all right, never mind. Good night, doctor.

(He hangs up the phone and shivers. He takes an old overcoat from a wardrobe and pulls it on. Then he picks up the head, lifts the dummy in the bed and puts the head back on, chuckling. The dummy is some kind of stage prop—life-size, with solid legs, but the rest stuffed with sawdust and straw. At present, it is dressed in a woman's nightdress—an expensive, diaphanous one. He looks at the ceiling, and caresses the dummy)

Yes, my darling. The beast and the lamb. *(He sits on the side of the bed and kisses the dummy)* Yes, my darling. Did you enjoy that? Did I stop too soon? *(He looks at the ceiling. With a sudden gesture of revulsion, he hurls the dummy away from him)* Agh! Women! All the same. *(Sitting on the edge of the bed, he stares into space as if hypnotized)* With their sweaty hands and wet lips and their hungry bodies. I should have married you. Yes, I should have married a dummy. Or an imbecile, like the man in the story by Maupassant . . .

5

(He shudders) Maupassant! *(He looks around nervously)*
But that was general paralysis of the insane . . . *(Suddenly jumping up)* I've been married to three women,
and all of them devoured me! And all were unfaithful! *(He goes over to a large, high-backed leather arm-
chair that faces the audience—it is a little like a throne.
He sits in this in a stiff, unnatural position, his fore-
arms along the arms of the chair, as if he were a crim-
inal about to be electrocuted)* The women are killers.
Vampires. *(He begins doing strange things with his right
hand again—stretching the fingers stiffly, holding his
hand in front of him as if it were a striking snake)*
But Harriet—she was the worst. *(Suddenly, his stiff,
tense face relaxes. He opens his eyes and smiles; he looks
almost friendly. Then he says, with cool deliberation)*
Why, you evil, sexy, cunning little bitch. How long do
you think you could take me in with your demure ways?
*(He is looking fixedly at the dummy—obviously imagin-
ing that it is* HARRIET*)* Women are so incredible! *(He
stands up, laughing gaily, and walks across the room)*
Such liars! And yet she wanted to play my Swanwhite,
the fairy child. *(Laughs)* The treasures of the humble!
What did you ever know about humility? You're more
like Miss Julie. Or Laura. Or Judith. *(Suddenly address-
ing himself, in a perfectly sane and composed manner,
to another chair in the room)* Well, my dear Steinmetz,
just look at her. What do you think? A sweet, modest,
beautiful young girl, eh? Miss Harriet Bosse, the first
Swanwhite. Look at that oval, childish face, those tiny
breasts, those straight little shoulders. What a darling!
What a baby! What a saint! How could any man want

to desecrate that white little body with his fumbling hands? Mmm? (*Turning and wandering back across the room*) Well, let me tell you the truth about the virginal Miss Bosse. I needed someone to play the part of the Lady in my *Road to Damascus,* and Palme suggested this unknown young girl—a girl I had never seen. I knew nothing about her except that she was eighteen, Norwegian, and that she'd played Puck in *A Midsummer Night's Dream.* Well, I interviewed her and gave her the part, although she seemed rather inexperienced. A few months later I went to the first dress rehearsal. And then there occurred the inexplicable scene. At the end of the first act, I went onstage to advise her about the kissing scene. We stood there in the middle of the stage, surrounded by a lot of people, and I was talking about the kiss, and looking down into her face. (*He stops as if astonished, then goes on slowly*) And as I talked, her face grew larger. It became supernaturally beautiful. Her eyes turned into a kind of luminous darkness, and I felt myself being *pulled into it.* (*He snaps his fingers*) And then, quite suddenly—and to everyone's astonishment— she turned and ran away. (*Slowly, almost hypnotically*) She turned and ran away . . . and I stood there, feeling that a miracle had happened. Why a miracle? Because, my dear Steinmetz, in the midst of all those people, she had given me a passionate and intoxicating kiss! And not a soul was aware of it! What do you say to that, eh, Steinmetz? A strange occurrence, don't you agree? (*Maliciously, to the dummy*) But there's even stranger to come—isn't there, my little virginal sweetheart? Why don't *you* tell him about it? Tell him about how you

7

came to my room. *(To* STEINMETZ*)* At first, she simply made me feel her presence. I knew she was there all the time, in my room. For three days. And then, on the third night, I had a dream about her. She came to me in her green Puck's costume, and when I undid the buttons . . . no breasts, none at all! And do you know what she did then? She gave me her foot to kiss! *(As if* STEINMETZ *had spoken)* Oh, yes, that was certainly a dream. But what happened the next night wasn't. She came to my bed naked. She removed my pajamas. And *(Trium-phantly)* she seduced me. And what is more, my dear Steinmetz, I happened to know that on that very night she had gone to visit her aunt in Uppsala. She seduced me at a distance of thirty miles! And so you see, Steinmetz, there can be no possible doubt that she is a witch . . . In the following May, we were married. By that time, I had possessed her thirty times. And yet on our wedding night, I discovered she was a virgin. How do you explain that, if not by witchcraft? *(Thoughtfully, to the dummy)* Yes, in the Middle Ages, they'd have burnt you. Perhaps they should still burn you. *(To* STEINMETZ*)* Another one of her favorite tricks was to fill my mouth with roses —the taste of roses. When that happened, I knew what it meant—that she'd be visiting me in the night. *(He flings himself into the chair again and takes up his "elec-trocution" position. He closes his eyes and listens, as if* STEINMETZ *is talking)* No, my dear doctor, I don't in the least mind you calling me mad. Why should I? It proves you still respect my sanity. After all, no one bothers to tell a genuine madman that he's mad. You just humor him. *(Sitting up and pointing his finger at* STEINMETZ, *speaking in a cool and reasonable voice)* But if it was some kind of hallucination, how do you explain that she never visited me during her menstrual period? . . . Oh, yes, I'm quite certain. I made a note of the dates when she didn't come, and after our marriage, I checked on them. She keeps a diary too, so it wasn't difficult. How do you account for that? Second sight? How did I know the exact dates if it was hallucination? *(Standing up again)* Ah, you simply don't understand, my dear doctor. This teacher of yours has filled your head with a lot of silly materialism. But allow me to say that there are certain matters upon which even Doctor Freud may be ignorant. For the past ten years I've been having experiences that Freud wouldn't begin to understand. They started in the Hotel Orfila in Paris. It was then I realized that I'd offended some unknown power. There could be penance, but no forgiveness. *(He listens, as if STEIN-METZ is speaking, then replies gently)* My friend, you are mistaken. I do *not* believe that all the women of the world are involved in a plot to destroy me. That is a stupid lie you've picked up from the fools who criticize my plays. I believe it is the nature of a woman to destroy men, just as it's the nature of caterpillars to destroy cabbages. And that is because a woman is incapable of love. It is the man who loves, the woman who accepts his love. The man kisses, the woman allows the kiss. A woman never gives herself; she only sells herself. But no, that is not quite true. A married woman sometimes gives herself to a lover, because it gives her pleasure to steal from the husband. But she never gives what is her own. She only sells it. And if a married woman wants revenge on her

9

husband, she gives with both hands, gives herself to
friends or to strangers . . . If I had known that from the
beginning, I would have saved myself a lifetime of suffering. If the men of the world knew the truth about women, they would stop making war on one another, and
turn their rifles on the women.

(*From the empty chair—which is turned away from
the audience—*STEINMETZ'S *voice speaks*)

STEINMETZ   Don't you think that's rather an exaggerated
view?

STRINDBERG   Possibly. But it's fundamentally true. Every
woman I've loved has betrayed me. No man has ever
betrayed me—not even my enemies . . . Yes, a man who
fights other men is a fool. That's just what women love.
Take Baron Wrangel, the husband of my first wife. Or,
no, take an even better example, Ina Forstén, the woman
who introduced me to the Wrangels. One day I was sitting in the Royal Library—you know I was a librarian
once—when a messenger brought me a letter. It said:
"Meet me punctually at five o'clock this afternoon before
number 65 Parliament Street. You will know me by the
roll of music in my hand." That was all. Brief. Imperious,
you see. No signature. I thought: Surely this is some
beautiful and romantic young girl who has seen one of
my plays—I'd written a couple of short plays in those
days. I thought: Yes, she must be an aristocrat, used to
giving orders. So I decided to go. And what did I meet?

(*As he speaks, the figure of* INA FORSTÉN *becomes
visible at the back of the stage.* STRINDBERG *gestures
towards her*)

A woman of uncertain age—between twenty-nine and forty—fantastically dressed. In short, a bluestocking. Well, she introduced herself as the fiancée of an old friend of mine, an opera singer called Algot Lange. She was in Stockholm for a week or so and wanted me to "take care" of her. "I, take care of a young woman!" I said. "Don't you know that I'm supposed to be the devil incarnate?" (INA *comes close to him as he speaks, and smiles seductively. She is by no means as repulsive as he represents her*) And at this she gave me a tender and patronizing smile, and said: "Oh, no, you only think you are. I know you thoroughly. You're just lonely and unhappy. You ought to try to stop being so morbid and gloomy." (INA *has sat in his chair, and looks up at him as he speaks, showing a slim leg and pretty foot.* STRINDBERG *goes on indignantly*) She was one of those obstinate creatures who strive to gain influence over men by insinuating themselves into the hidden corners of their souls. She kept up a large correspondence, bombarded all her acquaintances with letters, gave advice and warning to all young people, and knew no greater happiness than to direct and guide the destinies of men. Greedy of power, head of a league for the salvation of souls, patroness of all the world, she had conceived it her mission to save me! She chattered along like a bird, twittering incessantly. She had a completely empty head, no intelligence whatever, and a colossal impudence. Finally I got tired of her seriousness, so I began to tease her, making fun of everything—the world, men, religion, love, ambition.

(*By this time,* INA *has grown impatient of this tirade, and has stood up and walked around the back of the chair. Now, crossing the room, she snaps*)

INA   Oh, do stop it! Your ideas are completely morbid.

STRINDBERG   Morbid! My dear lady, my ideas morbid! They are, on the contrary, most healthy and up-to-date. But what about yours, now? They are relics of a past age, commonplaces of my boyhood, the rubbish of rubbish. And you think them new? Candidly speaking, what you are offering me as fresh fruit is nothing but preserved stuff in badly soldered tins. Away with it! It's rotten! And don't protest. You know exactly what I mean . . .
    (INA *turns her back to him, and during his subsequent lines, she prowls around the back of the stage, pouting, poking inquisitively at things with her umbrella.* STRINDBERG *continues, with self-satisfaction)*
    She left me without a word of goodbye, so furious she couldn't control herself. And then *(Now he becomes gloomy, and* INA *turns to him with a triumphant and sarcastic smile)* then she wrote to me again . . . and we met again, and this time she had the sense not to provoke me, so that I began to think she wasn't so bad after all. We paid a visit to her fiancé's aged mother, we took long walks in the park, I accompanied her on shopping expeditions . . . *(As he says this, he becomes less and less willing to speak. The words have to be forced out of him. Meanwhile,* INA's *smile broadens. He keeps his back turned to her, refusing to look at her. He bursts out)* It was incredible! The sheer stupidity of human nature! How can I explain it? I knew she was a conceited and empty-headed fool *(With a kind of groan)* yet within a week I was in love with her. Yes, laugh. I deserve it. But you see now why I've devoted my life to trying to

explode this stupid romantic fallacy about love? Everything about her annoyed me. I didn't like the drawling way she spoke, I didn't like the way she dressed, I didn't like the way she laughed. (INA *sits down on the floor as he speaks*) We used to stroll in the park every day, and she'd sit down on the grass, and then lie in provocative positions. (INA *does so,* STRINDBERG's *eyes encounter her breasts, which stand out sharply as she places her hands behind her head, and he looks away quickly as if scalded*) I knew she was a flirt. And at last I wrote her a letter confessing that I loved her. And do you know what she did? She sent it to her fiancé in Finland! And he wrote me a violent letter threatening to shoot me when he got back. (INA *is convulsed with laughter as he says all this*) And she was delighted! Two men loved her! They were threatening to kill one another! Splendid! She adored it. (INA, *lying on the ground, flings open her arms in a gesture of ecstacy, and opens her legs slightly as if inviting him to possess her. He shouts at her*) She was a flirt, a man-eater . . . a . . . chaste polyandrist, a professional *demi-vierge*. And then, when she was sure she'd got me, when she was sure I was caught and squirming in her web, she went away, back to Finland, back to her fiancé. (INA *stands up gracefully, brushes the grass off her skirt, glances at her face in a pocket mirror, then reaches out for his arm. He offers it automatically, then recoils angrily. With a slight shrug, she walks off.* STRINDBERG *is too preoccupied with his own tantrum to notice her absence. He clutches his head, looks as if he is tempted to bang it against the wall, and groans*) Ah, fool, idiot, imbecile, moron! Absurd, infatuated, gullible, childish, muddle-brained dolt! *How* could I have been so stupid?

STEINMETZ   Come, come. It's not as bad as all that. You didn't marry her, after all.

STRINDBERG *(With a cackling laugh)*   No, I suppose that's one consolation. Poor old Lange got her in the end. You can't pretend she wasn't cunning, playing one off against the other like that. Where I was concerned she only made one mistake—leaving me to go back to Lange. You see, he was already crazy about her. She'd got him like that. *(He waves a clenched fist)* She should have waited until the germ really got into my system. As it was, the fever began to abate as soon as she vanished. *(Suddenly becoming gloomy again; he turns sharply—a typical gesture—and thrusts his hand into his breast in the manner of Napoleon, then takes two strides across the room)* And yet all the same, she was the cause of all the misfortunes in my life.

STEINMETZ   Eh? How was that?

STRINDBERG *(Standing, looking out of the window, pointing)*   It was down there, in Drottninggatan, that she introduced me to her friend Baroness Wrangel—Siri von Essen. It was in front of that big lighted shopwindow there. And once again, the jaws of the trap opened. And once again, I marched into it like a soldier in a parade. And this time I marched straight ahead, without looking to right or left.

STEINMETZ Love at first sight . . .

STRINDBERG Oh, by no means. When I met her, I was
dazzled by her, but I no more thought of falling in love
with her than—than of falling in love with the queen.
She was far above me in social rank. You know I'm
merely the son of a maidservant and a bankrupt. She was
the wife of a baron who was a member of the king's
guard. In fact, I'd seen her husband once already. That
was when I marched with the students in the insurrec-
tion of 1868. He was standing on the steps of the monu-
ment in his dark-blue uniform, embroidered with yellow
and silver, with his little mustache and blue eyes and
pink cheeks . . . And I heard him give orders to the
soldiers to fire on the mob—on us, that is. And just as
the soldiers were loading their rifles, a king's messenger
rode up and ordered them not to fire. Mind, I didn't
know who he was until I met him with his wife. (*He
turns, reminiscently*) I thought his wife was a goddess.
She was the most beautiful creature I had ever seen.
They'd been married for three years, and her great ambition was to act on the stage. Since he was an officer in
the Imperial Guard, this was impossible, of course. But
they'd both read my plays and liked them. And they
were rather bored and lonely. So she invited me to her
house, and I went to call the next day. I thought the
address in Norrtullsgatan was slightly familiar when she
gave it to me. When I arrived, I knew why. It was the
house in which I had spent the unhappiest years of my
childhood. You see, an omen! The fates were trying to
warn me that nothing but misfortune could come out of

entering this house again. And yet I was so bored and lonely myself that I didn't care.

STEINMETZ   And can you tell me how long it took you before you decided you were in love with her?
(He is evidently making notes in a book)

STRINDBERG   Oh, I wasn't in love with her at that early stage. I adored her. I worshiped her. And I can tell you exactly when that began. In the summer, she decided to go to Finland for a holiday—her family was Finnish. One evening in June, I called to say goodbye. The servant told me she was in the garden. As I entered the courtyard, I saw her standing behind the garden railings. She was standing in the shrubbery, with her little daughter at her side. They were both dressed in white, and her brooches and bangles of alabaster seemed to throw a soft light over them, like lamplight falling through a white globe. The broad green leaves made her face seem death-like, as if she came from another world.

(The image of SIRI *and her daughter appears dimly in an alcove at the back of the stage as he looks at it, but the sight makes him shudder and turn away, at which* SIRI *disappears instantly)*

I was shattered, utterly confused, as if I'd had a vision. The instinct of worship that had always been latent in me now awoke. The void which had once been filled by religion ached no longer. The yearning to adore had reappeared in a new form. God was deposed, but his place was taken by the woman. Woman who was both virgin and mother. When I looked at the little girl, I couldn't understand how the birth had been possible, for she was obviously incapable of sexual intercourse. It was impossible to imagine her lying naked in a man's arms, because she was made of marble and sunlight and clear water. Yes, even when I looked at her husband, I failed to understand it. He also seemed completely noble and pure. Their union was essentially spiritual.

Can you understand my feelings? My life had been full of bitterness and nihilism. I was an atheist and a rebel, but I derived no pleasure from it. The world had always seemed to me an unpleasant and boring place, populated by mean-spirited imbeciles. I felt that life was meaningless, that all emotions were illusions, that man was a biological accident. And now, suddenly, everything was changed. I had something to look up to, to adore. I felt: These people shouldn't be living here in this house of misery. They should be living in the midst of woods and mountains, naked like gods. (With a sweeping circular gesture of both arms, and an infectious laugh) And suddenly the world was astonishingly beautiful. I felt as if I were seeing things for the first time—the sky, the trees, the view of the harbor out of my window. I began to feel tolerant toward my fellow men. I began to think: Well, they may be fools, but they're well-meaning. And if a man was obviously too vile to be excused, I thought: What does it matter? He's more to be pitied than blamed, because his meanness prevents him from seeing how beautiful everything is. And so, for a few weeks, I became a lover of men. I experienced a kind of rebirth. I hope you understand that this passion had nothing of the physical in it. I only wanted to sacrifice myself, to suffer without hope of any other reward but the ecstacies of worship, the self-sacrifice of suffering. I constituted myself her guardian angel. I wanted to watch over her, lest the power of my love should sweep over her and engulf her. I avoided being left alone with her, in case she came to suspect my passion. Besides, I was afraid that her husband might resent a familiarity between us. And above all, I was terrified of polluting her with my love. I felt it exerting a definite psychic pressure *(He makes a gesture to indicate his brain throwing off rays of energy)* so that she could hardly remain unaware of it if we were left alone for any length of time. *(He gives a sharp, barking laugh)* And the incredible irony of the whole thing was that she believed I was in love with Ina Forstén, who now seemed to me infinitely repulsive. I remember just before she left for Finland, she found me alone one evening, looking at a photograph of herself and Ina that stood on the piano. She came up softly behind me, and said: "You love her very much, with all your heart, don't you?" I nearly screamed with laughter. But I was afraid of giving the game away. So I stared at the photograph—at Siri's own face—and answered truthfully: "I worship her." And then felt like suicide for the rest of the evening.

When she sailed for Finland, the Baron proposed that we should go with her as far as the last customs station. So at ten o'clock the following evening, we met on board the steamer. It was a clear night. The sky was a blaze of orange, and the sea was calm. Then we steamed out slowly past wooded shores, in a light that was neither night or day, but had the qualities of both. You can

imagine that I was in heaven—standing beside my goddess as we steamed past little wooded islands. All three of
us were in a state of exaltation. We clasped hands and
swore eternal friendship. We declared that it was fate that
had brought us together. She begged me to take care of
her husband while he was away, and as I looked at him,
he seemed so handsome and noble that I wasn't sure
which of them I loved the most. Then, after midnight, our
mood changed. To tell the truth, we were all pretty tired.
I'd been ill, and I now began to feel cold. She treated
me like a sick child and made me sit down, and wrapped
her rug around me, and touched me with a mother's
tenderness. (*Closing his eyes, with immense feeling*)
Oh, god, it was agony! To feel her hands, to feel her
tenderness, when I was wrought up to such a pitch of
mystical adoration—it was more intense than any sexual
delight I had ever experienced. I didn't desire her. I
wanted to *be* her. I wanted her blood to flow in my veins.
I would have liked to dissolve her in water and drink
her. (*Trying to laugh, but failing, so that it is more of a
sob*) The pain and ecstacy were so intense that I felt
I was becoming transparent, that my body and soul were
tearing apart . . . It was one of those experiences that you
remember always as the most intense of your life. You
feel that the fates have all agreed to declare a truce with
you, to treat you as a favored child. I let my imagination
pour out in words, and I had a feeling that I couldn't
say anything wrong, that everything I said drew us closer
together. I could have confessed to a murder that night,
and I think they would only have loved me more deeply
for it . . . (*With an effort, he pulls himself together,*

forces himself into a lower key) Ah, yes, my dear Steinmetz, it's in moments like these that we catch a glimpse
of what man is striving to become, of a time when the
imagination burns with such a fierce flame that the flesh
is transmuted into spirit. Moments like these perform
an alchemy on a man's soul, so that he becomes more
than human.

Well, it came to an end. I sometimes wonder what
would have happened if that night had lasted twice as
long. We'd reached such a pitch of intensity that fatigue
seemed impossible. Would I have killed myself in sheer
exaltation? Ah well . . . the speculation is pointless. Dawn
came, the bay seemed to be swimming in flames, the
branches of the pines glowed like copper, and we looked
at it all as if we'd just arrived from Mars. And then the
pilot cutter arrived, and it was all over. The Baron and I
said goodbye to her, I kissed her hand, and then we were
headed for the shore. Six hours later, we were back in
his home, with our eyes so red and swollen that we hardly
dared to look at one another. I slept until midday on the
settee, covered with his military cloak. And for the next
few days we were together constantly, acting out our
blood-brother fantasy.

Still, the flat truth was that we were totally unalike. He
was a decent man, but fundamentally he was a military
idiot. He didn't really understand me, and I didn't understand him. We were as different as a horse and an ele-
phant. *(He suddenly begins to laugh)*

And the joke of it was that the Baroness had gone to
stay with Ina Forstén, and thought it her duty to plead
my cause! The incredible blindness of women! And after

a few days, she wrote me a letter assuring me that Ina wasn't really in love with her opera singer, that she thought constantly of me, and was thinking of returning to Stockholm to be with me again. *(He gives an exaggerated shudder and a shrill laugh)* Can you imagine anything more stupid and grotesque? My guardian angel was in love with me! This monster! This hideous man-eater of a bluestocking! The very thought of her filled me with horror. I even derived a sort of morbid satisfaction from thinking about her and imagining what it would be like to be tied to her for life! I remembered the sallow Mongolian face and red arms. I derived a vicious pleasure from remembering her seductive little tricks—her way of pulling out her watch so that she revealed a dainty bit of underclothing. I recalled the horrible day when I almost fell beyond recall. She was sitting in the midst of some bushes, with her skirt spread out around her, looking at me with an expression of childlike innocence. And I was about to lean over and kiss her . . . when my eyes fell on her feet, which were disfigured with bunions—and the spell broke. I used to remember this and break out in a sweat at the thought of what would have happened if she hadn't been stupid enough to take off her shoes . . . *(Shudders)* Ugh, my god! The abysses we avoid by an accident.

Well, the illusions began to collapse, one by one. I had to face the fact that the Baron and I were not really soul mates. And then, one day, I began to suspect that he kept a mistress! It was a shattering revelation! It happened one day when he had returned from the country. He'd been staying with his wife's cousin and her parents. I didn't know much about this cousin, except that everyone called her "Baby," and she was supposed to be charming and innocent. Well, I met the Baron in the street, and we went into a café to share a carafe of wine. And I found him almost unrecognizable. There was a kind of gay, dissipated look on his face. He was behaving like the hero of a comic opera—full of jokes and high spirits and sly *double entendres*. And when we'd had supper, he suggested we call on some female acquaintances of his, and I pretended I had an appointment and left him. For a few hours, I didn't know whether I was on my head or my heels. Then I began to understand, and it all seemed obvious. Of course this was why she struck me as so virginal and melancholy! Her husband was continually unfaithful to her! This empty-headed soubrette of a female cousin was his mistress.

The next time we met, he confirmed this. He was evidently determined to make a confidant of me. He told me that his wife was naturally frigid, but that she loved him and allowed him every freedom where other women were concerned. All this seemed incredible to me, yet it only confirmed my opinion of her as a goddess who was completely beyond his degraded understanding.

STEINMETZ And this, of course, was the point where you began to think about supplanting him?

STRINDBERG Not at all. You utterly fail to understand the nature of my romanticism. It was essential to my dream that she should be another man's wife. This meant that I could give my imagination full play without any fear of reality contradicting it. And yet reality began to break in, little by little. When Siri came back from Finland, she looked radiant and beautiful, but I soon began to notice there was something wrong. At first I didn't suspect it had anything to do with me. I knew they had some financial worries—he was a spendthrift—and she thought she could solve them by going on the stage. But of course, this was impossible for the wife of an officer in the king's guard. I assumed that this was the cause of her fits of melancholy. Then one day she announced she was taking her small daughter to the country for a month. It struck me as rather odd—she'd only just got back from Finland —but it was none of my business, so I said nothing. Two days after she left, the Baron sent for me and told me she was coming back immediately. He struck me as nervous and strange, and I didn't like the way he kept looking at me—slightly troubled and suspicious. He said she'd written him a rambling letter, in which she kept mentioning me—she said she was afraid I'd be angry with her. I told him it was absurd. What reason had I to be angry? A few days later, I called again and found her alone. And it was on this occasion that we had our first quarrel. She said: "Do you know that Gustav is angry with me for coming back unexpectedly?" I said I knew nothing about it. She gave me an odd look and said: "Then you don't know he'd been looking forward to meeting my charming cousin on his free Sundays?" And then . . . something happened. I can't explain it. I knew this was the moment for me to assume the role of confidant, to let her pour her woes into my ear, to take her hand and listen with a look of deep sympathy. And something . . . perverse in me refused to let me do it. Instead, I said: "My dear madam, if you want to bring charges against your husband, hadn't you better do it in his presence?" She looked as if I'd slapped her face. Then she became angry and said: "How dare you! Are you trying to insult and humiliate me?" And I was overcome by a kind of demon, and replied: "Yes, Baroness, I am insulting you." And then I left her and went home, feeling as if I had fallen from a great height and broken all my bones. Alone! I was alone! I'd worshiped her for months, and now her temple stood empty. I couldn't get used to the feeling.

STEINMETZ   Very understandable, of course.

STRINDBERG   You *don't* understand. It wasn't simply a feeling of desolation. The statue of the madonna had fallen down. *Woman* had shown herself behind the beautiful image, treacherous and faithless, with sharp claws and a capacity for hatred that makes men seem like good-natured children! When she attempted to make me her confidant, she was taking the first step towards breaking her marriage vows. At that moment, the hatred of her sex was born in me. She had insulted the man and the sex in me, and I had to take the part of the husband against her.

   (*Almost in tears*)   Yet it was a nightmarish agony, like having a leg amputated without anaesthetic. I felt I was going out of my mind. I knew I needed some desperate remedy. So I went along to spend an evening at the club with some old friends—journalistic cronies that I hadn't seen for months. They were a kind of hell-fire club, who met in a room with an altar in the center, with a skull and a bowl of cyanide and a wine-stained Bible. They were a poor lot of devils, acquainted with love only in its lowest aspects. But I needed their company. So I got drunk and joined in their bawdy songs. And when they asked me to make a speech, I launched into a witty and vulgar diatribe against women, heaping insults on my madonna. It gave me a strange, bitter satisfaction, as if some boil had burst. Then I staggered home and slept like the dead. And the next morning, I got to the library before the others, and I found myself burning with sensuality. I had to keep imagining my desecrated madonna without any clothes. I took down a work on art that contained all the famous sculptures of nudes from Italian museums, and looked through its pages, trying to imagine which one of them would look like Siri without her clothes. Finally, I decided on Diana, the virgin huntress. Then I turned to other publications on art to find more pictures of her. And I stared at them in an agony of sensuality, imagining that they were Siri, and that I'd torn off her clothes. And now suddenly I no longer worshiped her. I just wanted her like a beast. I violated her a thousand times in my imagination.

STEINMETZ (*Who obviously has his notebook out*) Most interesting. A remarkable case of ambivalence and emotional transformation. I shall send an account to Freud.

STRINDBERG (*Laughing harshly*) I don't find it interesting now. I find it pathetic. I'd taken my head out of a noose . . . and stepped straight into a trap that snapped on my leg.

(He gives a pantomime of the teeth of a trap closing with tremendous force, biting through the flesh)

And then, after all my self-lacerations, the Baron called on me that morning to ask me to go on an excursion to the amateur theater at Södertälje! Not a sign in his face that he knew I'd quarreled with his wife. When I enquired after her, he said: "Oh yes, she seconds the invitation, naturally. It wouldn't be the same without you." He was radiant and in high spirits, full of jokes and sly comments. And then he mentioned that his wife's cousin would be in the party—the famous Baby! So that was it! Whether I liked it or not, I was being cast in the role of the comforter of his wife! Incredible! From then on, it was like a runaway cart going downhill. Nothing could stop it. I had a sense of being a pawn, a plaything in the hands of fate. As soon as I met Siri again, I had a feeling that we were two magnets being drawn towards one another. And she knew it as well as I did. When I walked beside her, I was aware of a magnetic current flowing from her body to mine. Her feet kept pace with my own in an uncanny way, so that when I hesitated, she hesitated too, as if we were a single four-legged animal.

STEINMETZ   And the cousin?

STRINDBERG   Oh, I've told you. She was exactly what you'd expect—a little tart. Pretty in a common way, very vivacious, with big innocent eyes and a way of saying rather naughty things as if she didn't know what they meant! Oh, she was just the Baron's type. A typical flirt, a teaser. What infuriated me was that I could see that

she was provoking the Baron into a state of sexual excite-
ment, and he'd work it out later on Siri—probably still
thinking about the other woman. I began to feel as if I
were going mad. At one point I determined to escape the
whole thing and go to Paris. I actually gave a farewell
party in my attic, and they all came—including my friend
Lange and his new wife, my detested bluestocking, and it
ended with Siri throwing her arms around my neck in
front of everyone and bursting into tears. The next day
I left on the steamer. But I'd only been at sea a few hours
when I knew I couldn't go through with it. I went up to
the captain and said: "Captain, if you don't put me
ashore at once I shall go mad." He took one look at me
and went pale, as if he were looking into the face of a
homicidal maniac. The sailors rowed me ashore immediately and put me down in the midst of woods. (*He
laughs hysterically at the memory*) I watched them row-
ing away, and then went rushing into the forest, scream-
ing profanities. (*Suddenly feeling that he is being melo-
dramatic, he chuckles and says*) And then I decided
to commit suicide by drowning myself, and took off
all my clothes. I went and stood on a rock overlooking
the sea and hurled myself in. The temperature must have
been close to freezing, and I almost lost consciousness. I
swam a few hundred yards out to sea—and then was
struck by an idea. Why not die comfortably in bed, of
pneumonia, with Siri shedding tears over me! I immediately turned and swam back to land. Then I chose
the most exposed rock I could find, and sat there in the
wind. When even that didn't seem cold enough, I
climbed to the top of a pine tree, where the icy air

scorched my skin like a red-hot iron. Finally, when I was convinced I'd contracted double pneumonia, I came down and dressed and then walked to the nearest village, where I had a summer cottage.

In the morning, I woke up feeling slightly tired, but otherwise sickeningly healthy. So I wrote the Baron a long letter explaining that I had been taken ill suddenly and put ashore, and told him that unrequited love was driving me insane. He assumed, naturally, that I meant Ina Forstén. (*Pressing his hand to his head and laughing*) Oh, madness, madness! What stupid, self-deluding idiots we are! Ah, well . . . Am I boring you?

STEINMETZ   But no! On the contrary!

STRINDBERG   Good. To come to the point . . . The whole thing was bound to come out sooner or later. And it happened a few weeks later, in the new year of 1876. I'd spent the evening with the Baron and Siri. The Baron's mistress was also present. So were a couple of old gentlemen—the Baron's father and uncle. Finally, the cousin said it was time to go home, and the Baron said he'd accompany her. Ten minutes later, the old gentlemen said good night too. And so Siri and I were alone. We sat in silence for a while, looking at one another. Then she asked me quietly what had made me decide to go to Paris. When I didn't reply, she said: "I believe it was the same reason that made me go to the country a few days after I'd returned from Finland." And then there was no need to say any more. Our secret was out. And, of course, nothing happened. That is the difference between real life and fiction. If I decided to put such a scene on the stage, I should need tears, whispered avowals, the first tender kiss . . . Instead, we were interrupted by the two old uncles—one was showing the other the way to the lavatory. And that was our great love scene! We said very little. We agreed, briefly, that it would make no difference to our relationship, that we would continue to meet as before. And I walked home feeling like an angel, shining with purity and excellent intentions! *(Savagely)* It couldn't last, of course! We didn't really intend it to! We merely wanted to extract the maximum titillation from the experience, to tease our senses with whiffs of the feast to come! We had little casual meetings outside the library, when we'd stroll along the street and allow our hands to touch for a moment. And then one day, at last, she agreed to visit me in my room. Oh, there was still no suggestion of vulgar intrigue. It was all to be kept on a most exalted spiritual plane. We agreed that we had to meet for a serious discussion about whether she should tell her husband. When she arrived, my floor was covered with papers—I was working on a book about Sweden's relations with China and the Tartars—and I was sitting on the floor. There was even some question that she might confess everything to her husband before she came. But she'd lost courage at the last moment. And so she came and sat on my floor, and pretended to be interested in my papers. And then I leaned over her and kissed her, and she allowed herself to swoon backward on the floor . . .

STEINMETZ   And so it happened at last?

STRINDBERG   Oh, by no means! We were enjoying our game of hide and seek far too much for that! No, we

made love like fully dressed angels. We both showed remarkable inventiveness. We sinned without sinning. And
she managed to give herself without receiving. *(Laughs
harshly)* And then we stood up again, contented, happy,
without remorse, like angels who have not fallen. It was
that evening that I discovered that the pleasure of sex
lie almost entirely in the imagination.

STEINMETZ   You mean they're a delusion?

STRINDBERG   That is a problem I have never solved. All I
know is that the whole love affair with Siri was a tissue of
delusions. You asked me the other day whether I was
always a pessimist and a misogynist. Now I can give you
my answer. I became a pessimist after a long and minute
consideration of all the evidence for both sides. Throughout those early days with Siri, I gave careful thought to
the idea that I might have been mistaken in my tendency
to distrust life. It was true that I'd had a miserable childhood, that I'd suffered injustice at the age of five, that
I'd seen my own father treated as an intruder in the house
of my mother, that every step forward in my life had
been accomplished in the face of the most agonizing
pains and disappointments. And in spite of all this, I was
inclined to bend the knee, to acknowledge the funda-
mental benevolence of the universe. And all because it
seemed to me that in Siri I had found the ideal soul mate,
the woman who could make me whole. On that evening
when she first came to my room, I wrote in my diary: "If
ever again I doubt the existence of a benevolent deity,
may God strike me dead." A few months more of such

happiness, and I'd have been calling myself a Christian and praising woman as the noblest work of God. And at this point, the fates set out to prove to me that I'd been a gullible idiot. One by one, every single ideal I'd conceived in the last months proved to be a sham. The magic turned into a place of corruption. And how did it all happen? I still don't know. Can you say at precisely what point a flower loses its freshness and begins to wither? All I know is that it started when she confessed our love to her husband. He behaved like a gentleman, of course. No—more than that. He behaved like a sentimental fool. He wept hot tears and abased himself in front of her. He didn't try to dissuade her from leaving him. He said he wouldn't dream of trying to separate us. He only insisted that we respect his good name and conduct ourselves with discretion. (*Sarcastically and furiously*) And then Siri tried to outdo him in nobleness and called herself a guilty woman and blubbered louder than he did. I felt so disgusted when I heard about it that I tried to back out. I sent him a letter saying: "I have caused trouble between you—why don't you forget me, and I'll forget you?" But that would have been too easy. That was the last thing they wanted—to be given back to one another. So the Baroness had hysterics and pretended to be dying, and I had to go and sit at her bedside and comfort her. And the Baron pressed my hands with tears in his eyes . . . Ugh, it was madness. There is no surgical operation as painful as the tearing asunder of family ties. All passions are let loose, all the uncleanness from the depths of the heart comes bubbling out. As soon as the rumor leaked out, relatives on both sides started to interfere. Siri's mother reproached me for seducing her daughter, and the father of the Baron's mistress ordered her to leave the house of corruption before she got involved! And so it dragged on for month after month, the endless legal squabbles. He wouldn't let Siri divorce him because of his army career and because he wanted to protect his mistress's good name. So we had to pose as the guilty parties and receive all the sly looks and sniggering innuendos. And since, of course, a woman is supposed to be incapable of seducing a man, I had to play the role of the vile seducer, the serpent who's wormed his way into the bosom of the happy family and stolen the sweets reserved for the husband. At last it was all over. One night she came to my flat and said: "At last, I belong entirely to you! Take me quickly! Prove to me that you love me!" And so, feeling slightly defensive and foolish, I offered the required proof. And afterwards, she lay on my sofa like a goddess, and cast furtive glances at me, half shamefaced, half provoking, until I began to wonder how many times she'd need reassuring before I was allowed to go to bed. And I found myself looking at her and thinking: Is this the woman for whom I wanted to commit suicide? Is this my chaste madonna? And in that moment, I made the shocking discovery that I'd mistaken a nymphomaniac for a vestal virgin!

STEINMETZ *(Mildly)* Surely you're exaggerating. She wasn't as bad as that.

STRINDBERG But she was! Admittedly her upbringing and her desire for female dominance prevented her from giving free expression to her sexual impulses. Why do you think she wanted to become an actress? Because she was tired of repressions. She wanted to give free reign to her sensuality. And that's precisely what she did as soon as she was sure of me. I tell you, my virgin goddess never existed, except as an unwilling product of schooling. I realized this on the day when I went to help her move out of the Baron's house. The whole place was in chaos, and she'd left her underwear exposed all over the room for the delectation of the removal men. And from the time she left her husband's house, I saw her nature change day by day. She loved having people around her to admire her—one poor devil of a lover wasn't enough. And once she'd made her debut in the theater, she became worse. She seemed to have an urge to kiss and caress anybody who came near her. She made love to her female friends. She made love to her maid. She even made love to her dog, a vile, slobbering, goggle-eyed little monster that used to make messes on the carpet every day. I noticed that she'd look at handsome young men in a speculative sort of way. One day we went out on a boat trip, and she sat in such a way that her dress kept blowing above her knees. There was a rather powerful young fisherman steering, and she had him pop-eyed. Finally he noticed me watching him and looked the other way. Then Siri began to devour him with her eyes, until I made a sudden movement to attract her attention. Then she said: "I was just wondering what a pair of boots like that would cost"—of all the outrageous and preposterous excuses! Nothing seemed to make any difference to her desire to be petted and caressed by everyone. Her small daughter fell ill with brain fever and died a few days later. For a few weeks she was miserable and behaved like the woman with whom I'd fallen in love. I didn't even care that she obviously blamed me for the child's death—I'd felt guilty about my part in separating them and was willing to accept the blame. Then the manager of the theater saw her looking pale and miserable, and asked her if she'd like to play the part of Camille. And within a few weeks, she was her old self again, kissing everybody in sight, leaving her clothes all over the place, and caressing her filthy spaniel that growled every time I came into the room.

STEINMETZ   All this recrimination is rather trivial. A man like you should be above it.

STRINDBERG *(Pulled up in the full flood of self-pity)* Yes, you're right. Trivial. *(Struck by this, he crosses to the window and gazes out)* The story of my life. I could have been one of the master spirits of the age. And I let myself be destroyed by triviality . . . But that's the story of that filthy nineteenth century. Why did it murder so many of us? Schiller and Novalis and Hölderlin and Byron and Shelley and Nietzsche—poor Nietzsche. He was a friend of mine, you know. He was destroyed by a woman too. A predatory bitch called Lou Salome. He fell in love with her but he was too shy to tell her. So he sent along a friend to tell her and ask her to marry him. *(A snarling laugh)* She married the friend instead. *(Suddenly going red in the face, his rage arising)* What right had she . . . ? He was a great man, one of the giants of the age. The women—they want to destroy us. No, it's not the women. It's the . . . *(He gestures vaguely)* forces behind history. There are strange forces . . . strange forces . . . and they want to destroy us. Or perhaps only to tear our souls apart, to flay us into strength. And they've selected the women as their scorpions—to sting us, to whip us, to lacerate the flesh and the soul. But if you poke a snake with a stick, it strikes at the stick; it can't help it. Why should human beings know better than a snake? If the fates use women to lash us into agony, can they blame us for striking out at the women? I tell you that in spite of my reputation as a misogynist, I've devoted my life to the worship of woman. No man believed more devoutly than I that the "eternal woman draws us upwards and on." And I'm not speaking simply of Goethe's *"ewige weibliche."* There's a sexual truth that goes deeper than any idealism. There is a fire that burns beneath a woman's clothes, pulling the man towards her. And it has nothing to do with the personal. It's completely impersonal. Their silly human personalities only interfere with it. Why do you think I had to separate from my second wife, Frieda? Because I'd allowed myself to lose sight of that great truth. Siri was second-rate and brainless, so I thought I'd like to marry an intelligent woman who'd understand my work. It was sheer stupidity. Do you know that poem of Heine to an ex-mistress who wanted to keep up a Platonic friendship? It finishes:

> *Your body's love I still desire*
> *For it is young and fair.*
> *Your soul can go and hang itself,*
> *I've soul enough to spare.*

35

Well, that expressed my feelings about Frieda after we'd been married a month. Except that even her body became boring when I could make use of it at any hour of the day or night. Man has urges that carry him beyond the merely personal, and a woman can't understand a love that isn't personal. That was why I had to separate from Frieda. Six months after our marriage, I went to wave goodbye to her at the Gare du Nord in Paris. As the train pulled out she threw me a kiss and shouted: "We shall meet again soon." And I shouted back: "Soon." But as I turned away, I said aloud: "Never! Never again!" And then, with a feeling of wild joy, I rushed back to my room, and took my chemical apparatus out of a cupboard. (*He points to the table with retorts*) You see, I still have some of it. At the time, I had just become a famous writer in Paris. *The Father* had been presented at the Théâtre Nouveau, and everyone was anxious to invite me to parties. But in the sheer joy of separating from my wife, I thought only of chemical research. Oh, the ecstacy of locking the door of your room, of drawing the blind, of taking down a treatise by Mendeléeff, of preparing to explore the unknown. I worked throughout a whole day and night without sleep. And by dawn the next day, I had proved beyond all shadow of doubt what I had always suspected —that sulphur is not an element, that it contains carbon!

STEINMETZ Are you serious?

STRINDBERG Most certainly serious. In fact, I ended by demonstrating conclusively that sulphur is a combination of carbon, hydrogen and oxygen.

STEINMETZ *(Coughing)* Well, well. I'm no chemist, so I'm hardly qualified to judge. You certainly have remarkably wide talents.

STRINDBERG Pooh, that's nothing. A few months later I manufactured gold from lead and phosphate of lime. Unfortunately, I was only able to manufacture very small quantities. I also discovered a process for the manufacture of synthetic iodine, for which someone offered me a hundred thousand francs. I refused the offer and had the secret printed openly in a magazine. I considered that my discoveries belonged to the world. I wrote a botanical treatise to prove that the scientific classification of flowers is mistaken, and that all plants and minerals spring from a certain primary substance—

STEINMETZ Excuse me interrupting, my dear Herr Strindberg, but we were discussing the role of women in your life . . .

STRINDBERG *(Loftily)* The subject is unimportant. Why harp on it? You consider that my sexual adventures lie at the root of my misfortunes. I can tell you categorically that this is not so. *(Walking over to STEINMETZ's chair, then looking around nervously and at the ceiling)* I can now tell you the true secret of my life. My misfortunes all began when I started to practice black magic. From that day onward, the unknown spirits began to torment me. And from that time until the day I discovered the writings of Emanuel Swedenborg, they gave me no peace. I have been surrounded by spirits whose aim has been to force me to repent of my old materialism, to force me to swallow every scoffing word I ever wrote on the subject of religion—(*There is a light tap on the door, and he starts, then stares at the door with haunted eyes. Then he crosses quickly to the bed and takes the dummy in his arms. The door opens, and a pretty girl of about twenty looks in; she is wearing a dressing gown over a nightdress. With embarrassment*) Ah, Fanny. . . .

FANNY Excuse me, Mr. Strindberg . . . What on earth are you doing with that thing?
(*He throws it down awkwardly*)

STRINDBERG Er, nothing. I'm sorry. Am I keeping you awake?

FANNY Not me. Mama. She says it sounds as if you're having a party. She can hear voices . . .

STRINDBERG Yes . . . er . . . I was reading a new play aloud. But I'm sorry I kept your mother awake. Please apologize to her and tell her it won't happen again. I trust she's not too angry?

FANNY (*Stifling a yawn*) No. But she's a light sleeper. So if you wouldn't mind . . .

STRINDBERG Of course.

FANNY Good night.

STRINDBERG One moment. I wonder if you'd mind looking in the nursery?

FANNY   The nursery? What for?

STRINDBERG   I thought I heard a noise up there.

FANNY   There can't possibly be anybody there.

STRINDBERG   But would you look?

FANNY   Very well. (*She goes off, rather puzzled and obviously a little worried.* STRINDBERG *quickly goes to the door, waits until she is out, and goes after her. But, almost immediately, he darts back into the room and goes guiltily to the bed.* FANNY *comes back in*) Nothing, of course.

STRINDBERG   Did you look?

FANNY   (*Surprised at the absurdity of the question*)   Of course I looked.

STRINDBERG   You were very quick.

FANNY   Naturally. I only had to turn the light on and off.

STRINDBERG   How do you know she wasn't hidden somewhere?

FANNY   (*With astonishment*)   She?

STRINDBERG   (*Slightly embarrassed*)   Er . . . Harriet.

FANNY   What on earth are you talking about? You know

39

perfectly well she's in Helsinki with . . . *(She blushes and stumbles)* with her fiancé.

STRINDBERG *(Bitterly)* With Gunnar Castrén. You obviously know all about it.

FANNY It so happens that I do. I met her on her way to the station three days ago.

STRINDBERG *(Half to himself)* Everyone against me . . . But I thought you were on my side.

FANNY I'm on nobody's side. Anyway, I can assure you she's not upstairs. You probably heard a cat.

STRINDBERG There's a cat up there?

FANNY No.

STRINDBERG Then how can I have heard one?

FANNY *(Impatiently)* I don't know what you heard.

STRINDBERG *(Suddenly angry)* Don't you? Then why did it only take you a few seconds to look in the nursery? She could be hiding in one of the cupboards.

FANNY You're really quite mad! Or you've been drinking.

STRINDBERG *(Suddenly shouting)* Tell me the truth! Are you helping her?

FANNY *(Not angry, but a little frightened)* You've no right to speak to me like that!
(Her obvious sincerity brings him to his senses)

STRINDBERG *(With an effort at self-control)* I'm sorry. *(As she starts to turn away, self-pity breaks out)* You don't know what it's like to have everybody against you, to feel like a mouse . . .

FANNY *(Relenting a little, but still annoyed)* It's hardly surprising if you behave so strangely. *(With a touch of kindness)* You'll feel better in the morning. *(She turns and goes out. The kindness has been too much for* STRINDBERG; *it has touched off all his desire to confide in a woman)*

STRINDBERG *(Starting after her)* Fanny . . . *(But she has the sense to go. When he realizes this, he drops onto the bed and buries his face in his hands. Then he looks up with a sudden idea. Almost inaudibly)* Steinmetz? *(He moves to the telephone; but before he has lifted the receiver, he has already changed his mind. He drops it dejectedly)* No. Asleep. *(He crosses the room muttering)* Virgin goddess . . . Huntress. The cat and the mouse . . . *(For a moment, he stands electrified. Then he picks up a bottle of brandy from the table and pours himself a drink. He throws it back in one gulp, then smiles ironically)* Mad or drunk . . . There are worse spirits than come out of bottles.

(He flings off his coat and turns off the light. He throws the dummy across the room and flings himself into

bed. After a few preliminary sharp movements, he is asleep. Immediately, from behind the window curtain, there emerges a girl in a transparent nightdress. It is very obviously not FANNY; this one has long dark hair down to her waist, and an oval face. Her feet do not seem to touch the floor as she glides across the room. She bends over his bed, and seems to exude sensuality. He stirs uneasily, and his face turns up to her. She bends over and kisses him greedily; her hands stray under the bedclothes to caress him. Then, unable to restrain herself any longer, she slips into bed and throws the nightdress onto the floor)

Curtain

Part Two

SCENE 2

*The stage is in complete darkness except for a green iron
table on the left, upon which a spotlight is focused. In fact,
we are still in* STRINDBERG'S *room, and he is asleep in the
bed. What we now see takes place in his mind as he sleeps
uneasily. Behind the green table, the awning of a café is
dimly visible—this is Paris in 1894. There is a bottle of
champagne on the table.* HARRIET *is sitting there, looking
very beautiful and well-dressed, with a parasol.* STRINDBERG
*comes in, dressed in a dinner jacket. He is waving a news-
paper,* Le Temps.

STRINDBERG   It's in! Feydeau's given it two columns. "The
most compelling theatrical experience of the decade," he
calls it.

HARRIET   Congratulations.

STRINDBERG *(Sitting down)*   Sorry, have I been away long?

HARRIET   Only a few minutes. May I see? *(She takes the
newspaper as* STRINDBERG *takes the bottle of champagne
and opens it.* HARRIET *reads)* "Brutal, bitter, savage, and
completely convincing! . . . With one stride he has out-

45

stripped Ibsen and Zola!" Well, your fortune's made!
Everybody reads Feydeau!

STRINDBERG Damn Feydeau . . . with all respect. What on
earth can have happened to Adolphe?

HARRIET He should be here in five minutes. Or perhaps
he's simply decided to leave us alone.

STRINDBERG In that case, let us drink to his continued
absence. *(He pours champagne, and they raise their
glasses)*

HARRIET And to your continued success. *(They drink.
STRINDBERG sinks into the chair with a sigh of relief)*
Tired?

STRINDBERG Tired, but intensely happy. I can hardly grasp
all that's happened in the last twenty-four hours.

HARRIET How does it feel?

STRINDBERG I'm thinking mainly about the rage of all my
enemies.

HARRIET Why think about them?

STRINDBERG Because they've been trampling on my chest
for years, and it's a relief to throw them off.

HARRIET Don't you find it strange to be sitting here alone
with an insignificant girl like me? When you ought to be

showing yourself in the cafés and playing the conquering hero.

STRINDBERG *(Disingenuously)* I prefer your company.

HARRIET You don't look as if you do.

STRINDBERG I feel . . . rather sad. A feeling halfway between nostalgia and melancholy.

HARRIET Why?

STRINDBERG Because I feel success has come rather too late. One should be successful at twenty-four, not forty-four. The nerves are too tired to enjoy it.

HARRIET *(Leaning towards him)* Would you like me to help you?

STRINDBERG There's nothing I'd like more.

HARRIET And what about your wife? Wouldn't she object?

STRINDBERG Oh, she hasn't even read the play. She's sitting at home, patiently waiting for me because our daughter has a slight chill. Mind, mind, she's good and considerate, and I'm really fond of her.

HARRIET But . . .

STRINDBERG She'd think it wrong to go out and celebrate like this tonight. I once treated her to a bottle of champagne, and do you know what she did? Picked up the wine list to see what it cost, and then burst into tears! Cried because she said Marion needed new stockings! *(Standing up impatiently)* No, a man needs a spark from a woman to set him dreaming and struggling, to show him what life can be. That's why any man of imagination's a sitting target for a vital and attractive woman. What's the point of being a conqueror unless there's a woman to admire your conquests?

HARRIET   But you've no need to be without a woman. Don't you know that the moment of success makes a man irresistible?
(She takes something out of her handbag)

STRINDBERG   What's that?

HARRIET   Only a laurel wreath. I meant to send it up to the stage, but I didn't get a chance. *(She goes to him and places it on his head, then stands on tiptoe to kiss his forehead. He recoils as if burned)* Hail, victor.
(She kneels in front of him)

STRINDBERG   Don't! Your terrify me!

HARRIET   How timid you are! You're afraid even of good fortune! Who took away your self-assurance and turned you into a pygmy?

STRINDBERG *(With pride)*   Not a pygmy. A dwarf, perhaps. I don't work up in the clouds like a giant, crashing and thundering; I forge my swords in the heart of the mountains. You think I'm too modest for the victor's wreath? No, I despise it because it's not enough for me. I dream of a conquest so complete that this petty success is a mockery, a parody. Damn those idiots in the theater and damn their applause. Tommorrow they'll be sneering at me if the mood takes them . . . (*Turning to her, and finding her eyes fixed on him with fascination*) But a woman's a reality, something I can't ignore. (*Throwing off the laurels*) I don't want this. I want my real reward . . . (*He moves towards her and she sways towards him*)

HARRIET (*Dreamily, hypnotized*) Take it. It's yours.
　　(*He kisses her*)

STRINDBERG Strange, what a relief it is to behave like a swine. When I saw you this morning, for the first time, I knew you'd be in my arms before the night was over.

HARRIET (*Impatiently*) Let's not stay here. Let's take the champagne up to my room.

STRINDBERG In ten minutes. We don't want Adolphe to arrive and find us gone.

HARRIET I thought that's precisely what you *did* want.
　　(*She laughs*)

STRINDBERG Does it give you pleasure—to make me betray my wife and my best friend?

HARRIET (*Laughing and pouring them more champagne*) I think you're the sort of person who can't enjoy yourself without feeling guilty and tormented. *(She hands him his glass)* Well, I don't feel in the least guilty about enjoying life. I accept it as my natural right. So will you when you've got used to being successful.

STRINDBERG If I have a chance to get used to it . . .

HARRIET Stop it! Drink your champagne. Look. *(She stands in front of him, thrusting out her breasts, her head held back)* Do you want me?

STRINDBERG Don't! You make me dizzy!

HARRIET I'm supposed to. Stop mistrusting life.

STRINDBERG Have you ever committed a crime?

HARRIET Not really. Nothing serious. I once killed somebody.

STRINDBERG Who?

HARRIET My father.

STRINDBERG Are you serious?

HARRIET *(Laughing)* In a way. Oh, it wasn't me alone: it was the whole family. I think we killed my father with hatred. You see, he had a terrible way of systematically opposing all our likes and desires, and where he found any real vocation or interest, he tried to destroy it. And so he aroused an opposition that turned into hatred, and in the end it grew so powerful that he pined away, lost his will power, and finally wished himself dead.

STRINDBERG   Did your conscience never reproach you?

HARRIET   No. In a way, we felt he'd brought it on himself, as if he wanted to die. He'd started to hate life.

STRINDBERG   How do you know it wasn't just people that he hated?

HARRIET *(Shrugging)*   Perhaps.

STRINDBERG   I once knew a man who tried the experiment of telling people the truth. Like all of us, he was surrounded by a circle of people he called friends, although they were the usual bunch of fools and rotters. Still, he needed company, so he put up with them. One day he gave a big party. It was the evening, and he was feeling tired. And suddenly he realized he couldn't go on concealing his thoughts and talking rubbish to his guests. So when it was his turn to propose a toast, he suddenly started to tell them what he really thought of them. He stripped every one of them naked, telling all he knew about their treacheries and meannesses. Then he sat down and told them all to go to hell. His wife started to scream at him and all the guests made a rush for the door. And the next day they had him certified and taken away to a madhouse. *(Laughs)* And they wouldn't let him out. They kept him there until the day he died . . .

I'm always expecting them to do the same to me. Oh, I know. It's happened before. In Stockholm ten years ago, they tried to suppress one of my books as obscene. I was in Geneva at the time. I could have stayed there, but they could still have put the publisher in jail. So I went back, expecting to be stoned. And instead a great crowd of cheering people met the train. They carried me on their shoulders to my hotel, and for the next three weeks I was the national hero, the defender of civil liberties, the spokesman of the liberals! Everybody was so anxious to canonize me that they conveniently forgot that the book was an attack on the feminist movement. And when the book was acquitted, they had torchlight processions and put on special performances of my plays, and the audience stood up and cheered at any line that sounded like an attack on authority.

HARRIET   How wonderful!

STRINDBERG   Not at all. It nearly ruined me. As soon as I left the country, all my supporters forgot me as quickly as possible, and all the people they'd antagonized— people who'd never heard of my name before—abused me in the newspapers and clamored for the suppression of my books. And my so-called supporters didn't have a word to say.

HARRIET   But it can't happen this time. This is Paris, not some stupid provincial city. Come on. Drink. (*She takes his arm, and tries to make him take the glass*) Let's go back to my room now.

(But STRINDBERG *is listening to voices from the past. He stands there, staring into the darkness, which is now becoming lighter. The light around himself and* HARRIET *is becoming dimmer. The* JUDGE's *voice is heard)*

JUDGE   Would the prosecutor read aloud the words complained of?

(As the light comes up we see the PROSECUTOR, *a strange-looking man—a compound of Ibsen and Strindberg's father: a man in his sixties, dressed in the manner of a burgher of the mid-nineteenth century)*

PROSECUTOR   Here they are, my lord. "The priests are adept at practicing fraud with Hogstedt's Piccardon burgundy at sixty-five öre the bottle, and Lettstrom's maize wafers at one krona a pound, which they declare to be the flesh and blood of the popular agitator Jesus of Nazareth who was executed over eighteen hundred years ago."

JUDGE   Has anyone anything to say about the defendant?

SIRI *(Appearing in the witness box)*   I am his first wife. I believe he was driven mad by reading the ravings of an atheist called Frederick Nietzsche.

JUDGE   What reasons have you for thinking so?

SIRI   After he began to correspond with Nietzsche, his whole manner changed. He began to talk about the superman all the time, and he developed a strange laugh. When our four-year-old son asked: "Can God see in the dark?" he said: "No, but daddy can."

JUDGE *(Suppressing a smile)*   I see. And are you a devout Christian yourself?

SIRI   Oh, no. But I just thought it was rather silly to take this attitude towards children. They're too young to make up their minds for themselves. And they might be glad of a little simple faith when they get older.

STRINDBERG *(Now speaking from the shadows on the other side of the stage, although his "body" is still in bed)* Don't go on about it! I acknowledge that it was stupid of me . . .

STRINDBERG *(As a defendant)*   I agree that Nietzsche's ideas went to my head at a time when I badly needed a little self-confidence. The battle against the philistines had almost wrecked my health. My plays were failures. Publishers rejected my books. My wife had lost her job in the theater. We had no money. Ibsen had held up my marriage to ridicule in *The Wild Duck*. And here, suddenly, I discovered a man who had the courage to say: "I am the most independent and perhaps the strongest mind living today." My self-belief woke up again. I wrote back: "Yes, you and I both!"

SIRI *(Interrupting)*   And then he became completely intolerable around the house. We were living in cheap rooms in a filthy old castle near Copenhagen. The children went about in rags; we had hardly enough food. And yet he'd fly into a tantrum if we didn't give him the food he liked or if his shirt hadn't been ironed. He used to shout some silly lines from Nietzsche about: "If you go to see a woman, don't forget your whip . . ." He constantly accused me of infidelity—even with my woman friends. Yet he seduced the daughter of the gypsy steward and got into an awful panic at the prospect of being thrown in jail for seducing a minor.

STRINDBERG (*Yelling with rage*) That's a lie! The girl made advances to me. And she was only technically a minor. She was nearly sixteen.

JUDGE Hmm, you seem to have had a rather eventful sex life.

PROSECUTOR (*Crisply*) My lord, I submit that the man is a sex maniac who has gone insane through constant brooding on sex. I would also like to produce Doctor Upvall to give evidence that he also had homosexual tendencies. I believe this also accounts for the extraordinary accusations he made against his wife and her woman friends.

STRINDBERG (*Frantic*) A lie! A monstrous and hideous lie!

PROSECUTOR (*Sharply*) A lie? Then will you tell me if you recognize the handwriting of this letter?
(*He waves a letter under* STRINDBERG's *nose*)

STRINDBERG (*Taken aback*) Yes . . .

PROSECUTOR And do you deny you wrote the following lines to Edward Brandes: "My spirit life has received in

55

its uterus a tremendous outpouring of seed from Frederick
Nietzsche, so I feel as swollen as a pregnant bitch. He is
my husband . . ." *(He reads the last part mockingly and
bitingly)* Is that the kind of image that would occur to a
completely masculine man?

JUDGE   Is the prosecutor alleging that Mr. Strindberg
had improper relations with Herr Nietzsche?

·   PROSECUTOR   No, my lord.

JUDGE   In that case, I think we'd better confine ourselves
to the facts. These accusations are beside the point.
    *(STRINDBERG glares triumphantly at the PROSECU-
TOR)*

PROSECUTOR   I beg to be allowed to clarify my point. I
submit that this man was never completely sane during
his whole life and that after his first marriage, he became
steadily more insane. I would like to call Doctor Steinmetz
to offer testimony on this point . . .

STRINDBERG   Steinmetz! You too!
    *(STEINMETZ enters the box, which SIRI quietly va-
cates. There is something oddly familiar about him. A
middle-aged psychiatrist with graying hair and the sober
dark suit of a medical man—yet the face is not at all un-
like STRINDBERG's. The same small beard, the same
pointed mustache. But the resemblance is not too marked)*

PROSECUTOR   Doctor Steinmetz, would you give us your
view on whether Herr Strindberg is insane?

5 6

STEINMETZ *(Pedantically)* To decide in general terms whether Strindberg is mentally deranged is pointless; for if, proceeding from a predetermined definition, one assumes mental derangement only when the individual loses his self-possession, his bearings and power to arrange his ideas, then Strindberg has never been mentally deranged. (STRINDBERG *grins delightedly, and bows ironically to the* PROSECUTOR) But he suffered from a well-known, characterizable process which occupied more than twenty years of his life—say from 1889 until the present day—and which one can call paraphrene, schizophrene or paranoiac. I have observed in him an abundance of incomprehensible, heterogeneous but recognizably coordinated symptoms . . .

PROSECUTOR Could you be a little more specific, doctor?

STEINMETZ *(Clearing his throat)* It is difficult in explaining to laymen, but I'll try. The subject had an exceptionally difficult childhood, since he was one of twelve brothers and sisters, five of whom died in earliest infancy. His mother, who was never particularly fond of him, died when he was thirteen. Like his father, the subject possessed a hypersexual temperament, which found outlet in the usual autoerotic activities. Unfortunately, he read a book that convinced him that these activities had doomed him to insanity and an early death. All of this tended to exaggerate and sustain his feeling of insecurity and mistrust.

JUDGE Mistrust of whom?

STEINMETZ Of life in general, at this point—of fate, if
you like. Dr. Freud has pointed out that a certain mistrust
of life is inevitable in all adolescents, since they are
uniquely self-centered and fail to grasp how far their self-
preoccupation is the cause of their misfortunes. But this
mistrust usually vanishes with adolescence, and the adult
man develops a realistic sense of cause and effect. Marriage is often an important factor in creating this mature
attitude, since it tends to be a matter of mutual admira-
tion. In the case of Herr Strindberg, his courtship of the
Baroness Wrangel was probably the closest he ever came
to complete sanity—that is, to losing his adolescent distrust of life. Unfortunately, he showed a certain lack of
judgment in his choice of a wife—as, in fact, he continued to do throughout his life. The Baroness was an
admirable woman, and I believe she was wholly in love
with her husband. But she had too much of a mind of
her own to be a suitable wife for a husband with . . . er
. . . so many fixed ideas. In my own opinion, this was the
worst thing that could possibly have happened to Herr
Strindberg at that point. He was more than half converted
to . . . er . . . shall we say, a more positive view of human
existence, when his disagreements with his wife convinced him that it was a mistake to trust anyone. From
then on, he was trapped in the vicious circle: general
suspicion and mistrust producing hostility in other people,
and the hostility deepening his own mistrust of the
world.

STRINDBERG My lord, may I ask the doctor a question?

JUDGE If it is relevant, yes.

STRINDBERG Doctor, would you regard a man who takes a pessimistic view of human affairs as insane?

STEINMETZ Not necessarily, but he can easily become so. Sanity is accompanied by a feeling that action is worthwhile. A pessimist who wants to improve things can remain perfectly sane. A pessimist who feels that nothing can be done is subjecting his sanity to a dangerous burden.

STRINDBERG May I ask if you have ever read the Book of Job?

STEINMETZ Of course.

STRINDBERG And the Book of Ecclesiastes?

STEINMETZ Yes.

STRINDBERG And Schopenhauer's *World as Will and Idea*?

STEINMETZ In part, yes.

STRINDBERG And Hartmann's *Philosophy of the Unconscious*?

STEINMETZ I have.

STRINDBERG And do you consider the writers of all these works insane?

STEINMETZ   You are distorting my words. Pessimism is not a synonym for insanity. But pessimism is nearly always a symptom of insanity—particularly of schizophrenia and paranoia.

STRINDBERG *(Angrily, to the* JUDGE*)*   All this talk is stupid and heartless. I could accuse myself of far more than you accuse me of. *(To the* PROSECUTOR*)* I could prosecute myself more effectively than you prosecute me. But all of this nonsense about insanity is neither here nor there.

PROSECUTOR   Would you tell the court what kind of self-accusations you have in mind?

STRINDBERG   Very well. I wanted my mother to die because she never took me seriously. Later, I thought how convenient it would be if Siri's daughter were to die. I didn't seriously want her to die. But I knew that Siri would never be happy with me while her daughter stayed with her husband—

PROSECUTOR *(Impatiently)*   This is hardly serious—

STRINDBERG   Let me go on. At the trial of my book I came to hate two of my persecutors and I wished them dead. This time I really *willed* it—I directed my hatred at them in a beam. Both of them died within a month. It was then that I realized that I possessed strange powers, and that, without intending it, I had probably murdered my mother and Siri's daughter. *(With a sinister smile at the* PROSECUTOR*)* Tell me, would you not agree that a man with a secret like that has a right to be a little insane?

PROSECUTOR *(Blandly)* Your so-called secret was nonsense. It is impossible to kill a man by willing his death.

STRINDBERG Are you sure?

PROSECUTOR Quite sure. But if the court wishes to test the hypothesis, I am willing to offer myself as a subject. *(Slowly and explicitly)* Try and will me to death.

STRINDBERG *(Nervously)* That is impossible.

PROSECUTOR Why?

STRINDBERG Because I'd succeed and bring further misfortune on myself.

PROSECUTOR Did your last . . . attempt bring misfortunes on you?

STRINDBERG Yes! It was the cause of all my misfortunes— what you call my madness.

PROSECUTOR Would you describe how this came about?

STRINDBERG It was after my second wife left me alone in Paris. Everything was going well. I had proved that sulphur is not an element, and that gold is a compound of iron and sulphur. I was never in need of money, although I had no source of income at the time. Whenever I needed it, money seemed to appear. And then, one day, a letter arrived from my wife awakening an intense desire to be reconciled with her. But how was this possible, since divorce proceedings had already been started? Then I had an idea—or the devil put it into my head. If our child were to fall ill, she would send me a telegram asking me to come to her . . . Now, I knew I possessed certain powers of telepathy. So I found a photograph of our daughter and brooded on it, willing her to fall into a fever. Not a dangerous one, you understand! I wished the child no harm.

PROSECUTOR *(With irony)*   And did it work?

STRINDBERG   It did, but not in the manner I intended. My other daughter fell ill—the child of my first wife, which, of course, was no good at all. And my attempt at witchcraft turned the invisible powers against me. From then on, misfortunes rained on me, and strange coincidences left me in no doubt that all this was intended to punish me.

PROSECUTOR   Strange coincidences? Would you describe some of them?

STRINDBERG *(Waving his hand vaguely)*   Well . . . I'll tell you how it all began. I was experimenting with the seed of a nut. I detached the germ and placed it under my microscope. It had a sort of heart-shape, rather like a pear. And then, when I peered at it through the eyepiece, I saw it as two tiny hands—human hands, completely white, like ivory—clasped together as if in prayer.

PROSECUTOR   Is there anything strange about that? Have you never seen a potato that looked like a human head?

62

STRINDBERG

STRINDBERG   You don't understand. This wasn't merely a
resemblance. They were perfectly sculptured hands, as if
they'd been carved by a Michelangelo. I ignored the
omen, of course, and went on practicing my black magic
with the photograph. This was before I knew my other
daughter had fallen ill . . .

PROSECUTOR   Ah, I see. This was an omen to try and make
you give up black magic?

STRINDBERG   Of course. And when I ignored it, the invisible powers really began to torment me. They left me no
doubt that it was deliberate. You see, I'd experienced
omens before, but they usually announced good fortune.
For example, on the morning when I began my experi-
ments to make gold, I happened to take a walk along a
street I'd never seen before. Suddenly, I found myself in
front of a laundry window on which was painted a trade-
mark—a silver cloud and a rainbow, and between them,
my own initials, A. S.! I knew immediately that my ex-
periments would be successful.

PROSECUTOR   One small point. You were christened John,
were you not?

STRINDBERG   (Haughtily)   John August.

PROSECUTOR   But throughout your childhood everyone
called you John?

STRINDBERG   Yes.

PROSECUTOR   Then the initials above the shop should have been J. S., should they not?

STRINDBERG *(Angrily, to the* JUDGE*)*   I refuse to answer questions that are a deliberate attempt to humiliate me.

PROSECUTOR   Very well. Let me forget it. But one more point, before you go on. The word August means "grand, majestic, awe-inspiring," does it not?

STRINDBERG   You know what it means as well as I do!

PROSECUTOR   Is that why you preferred it to "John"?

STRINDBERG   The question is impertinent.

PROSECUTOR   I ask the court to take note of the prisoner's curious sensitivity on these points.

STRINDBERG   I resent these innuendos!

PROSECUTOR   If you insist, I will state my meanings more plainly. (STRINDBERG *is silent)* Would you prefer it?

STRINDBERG *(Sarcastically)*   It would be an advantage to know precisely what I'm supposed to be accused of.

PROSECUTOR *(To the court)*   I submit, my lord, that the prisoner is an extreme case of delusions of grandeur. He has spent his whole life in an effort to force the world to acknowledge his claims to genuis. I suggest, my lord, that

August Strindberg is not simply a name, but a title: *August* Strindberg, the mighty Strindberg, who should have been born a king or an emperor!

JUDGE (*Mildly*) But I've been given to understand that the prisoner possesses a certain literary talent. Not that I've ever read any of his books. But I'm told he's quite highly regarded in Sweden.

PROSECUTOR As far as Sweden is concerned, my lord, that is flagrantly untrue. I would like to call the literary critic and historian Gustav Böök.

(*Enter* BÖÖK, *who also looks oddly like* STRINDBERG; *he enters the box*)

STRINDBERG You! Judas Iscariot!

BÖÖK (*Bowing to him sarcastically*) Jesus Christ.

JUDGE Hmmm. Could we try to maintain a certain level of dignity in these proceedings? (*To the* PROSECUTOR) Would you go on?

PROSECUTOR Herr Böök, you are the author of a general survey of Swedish Literature contained in the quarterly *New Sweden* for Autumn 1909. And yet the only recent play you picked out for commendation was Tor Hedberg's *Johan Ulfstjerna*. Have you read Herr Strindberg's work?

BÖÖK I have indeed.

PROSECUTOR   Would you tell the court your opinion of it?

BÖÖK *(Taking on a pedantic manner)*   Strindberg's work
falls into two periods: the period of realism, and the
period of fantasy—or expressionism, as some of our Ger-
man critics prefer to call it. It was his plays of the first
period that gained him a certain notoriety. *The Father,*
for example, is a play of great passion and force, but when
analyzed it turns out to be mostly sound and fury, signify-
ing nothing. It is about a virtuous husband whose wife
sets out to drive him insane by trying to convince him
that he is not the father of their child. I think I need
hardly dwell on the absurdity of this plot. I mean, upon
the fact that any sensible husband would simply divorce
his wife or leave her—particularly if she were the kind
of sexless monster that Strindberg portrays. Instead, the
play ends with the husband being dragged off in a strait
jacket and the wife gloating over his downfall. The whole
thing is so overstrained and hysterical that it is difficult
to take it seriously as a piece of drama. *The Father* was
written in 1887, and for the next ten years Strindberg
wrote almost nothing except a number of wild books on
alchemy and botany. Then he started to produce a series
of fantasies which, in my own opinion, are totally worth-
less. They are mostly symbolic accounts of Strindberg's
own life, and have no value except as fragments of dis-
torted biography. They are so completely subjective that
he might have written them in a private shorthand and
left them in manuscript. They are morbid, formless and
hysterical. In fact, the only person that they could possibly interest is a specialist in mental diseases.

STRINDBERG

STRINDBERG Tell me, doctor, have you ever read a novel
of mine called *Black Banners?*

BÖÖK *(Impassively)* I have.

JUDGE *(To* STRINDBERG*)* Would you mind explaining to
the court the significance of that question?
*(*STRINDBERG *grins maliciously at Böök)*

BÖÖK I presume what Mr. Strindberg means to imply is
that I have good reason for attacking his work, since he
satirized me recently in an extremely bad novel called
Black Banners about the literary life of Stockholm.

JUDGE And did he?

BÖÖK *(With sincerity)* I hope the court will accept my
word when I say that I have been unable to read more
than ten pages of the book, and have no idea of whether
I am included in its portrait gallery.

STRINDBERG Then how did you know I'd put you in it?

BÖÖK I didn't. I merely inferred it from your question. *(To
the* JUDGE*)* I should add, my lord, that Mr. Strindberg's
literary output has also included a number of curious
works that he calls novels, although in other places he
frankly refers to them as parts of his autobiography. He
made his reputation in 1879 with a satire on journalism
called *The Red Room.* My lord, I am attempting to be
scrupulously honest when I describe these works as in-

credibly bad. Like all Strindberg's work, they are full of self-pity, and the invective is so wild and hysterical that it leaves all its targets untouched.

JUDGE Hmmm, I see. Thank you, Professor Böök. Have you any more general remarks to make on Herr Strindberg's work?

BÖÖK No, sir..

JUDGE In that case, you may stand down.

PROSECUTOR Excuse me, my lord, I have a few more questions I would like to put to the professor. Doctor, your opinion of Herr Strindberg's work appears to be extremely low.

BÖÖK I'm afraid it is.

PROSECUTOR Would you agree that this is because Strindberg is so self-absorbed that he has never succeeded in creating literature?

BÖÖK Partly. Let me put it this way. Herr Strindberg's work is not merely too personal. It also seems to enjoy wallowing in the most painful emotions. When he is not accusing the world, he is accusing himself. And when he is not accusing himself, he is justifying himself.

PROSECUTOR Admirably put, doctor. Thank you. You may stand down. My lord, I would like to call the prisoner's first wife again. (SIRI *enters the box*) Now, Baroness, have you ever heard or read a play called *The Bond?*

SIRI   That vile thing! He should be whipped for writing it.

PROSECUTOR   Would you tell the court why you feel so strongly about the play?

SIRI *(To the* JUDGE)   It is a thinly disguised account of our divorce proceedings.

PROSECUTOR   Under what name are you represented?

SIRI   As the Baroness.

PROSECUTOR   And Herr Strindberg?

SIRI   He calls himself the Baron.

PROSECUTOR   Hmmm, another promotion . . .
        (*He looks at the* JUDGE)

JUDGE   I note your point. Proceed.

PROSECUTOR *(To* SIRI)   Would you mind describing the plot of the play?

SIRI   It has no plot. Its sole purpose is to justify himself and blacken me. He represents the Baroness as an adulteress and a self-confessed liar.

PROSECUTOR   Herr Strindberg, do you deny that the play is no more than an act of revenge on your wife?

STRINDBERG   It is intended as an attack on injustice.

PROSECUTOR   Hmmm, well, let us see how far it carries out that intention. My lord, I ask permission to read aloud a short passage from the play. We have asked this lady to read the part of the Baroness.
   (Enter FANNY. STRINDBERG *stares at her incredulously)*

STRINDBERG   Fanny! You!
   (She smiles at him with catlike malice)

PROSECUTOR *(Taking a book)*   And perhaps Herr Strindberg would oblige us by reading the words of the Baron?

STRINDBERG   I refuse.

PROSECUTOR   In that case, I shall read them myself.

STRINDBERG   You'll do nothing of the sort. I know how you'll distort them. *(He snatches the book, which is open, glances at it, then throws it aside)* I don't need this. I know my own play.

JUDGE   Very well. Proceed.

PROSECUTOR *(To* FANNY)   Now, Baroness, do you deny that you are the cause of the dissension?

FANNY *(In her role as the Baroness)* Yes, indeed I do. It takes two to make a quarrel.

PROSECUTOR Baroness, this is not a quarrel but a legal action. Moreover, you seem to me to be displaying a contentious disposition and an uncompromising attitude.

FANNY But you don't know my husband.

PROSECUTOR Please be more clear. This court cannot pronounce sentence upon insinuations.

STRINDBERG In that case, I ask that this suit may be dismissed so that I may seek divorce by other means.

PROSECUTOR The case is already before the court and must proceed. You assert, then, Baroness, that this is all your husband's fault. Can this be proved?

FANNY Yes, it can.

PROSECUTOR Then kindly do so, but remember that this will deprive the Baron of his rights both of fatherhood and property.

FANNY He has forfeited these many times over. Not least when he denied me food and sleep—

STRINDBERG As to that, I must explain that I have never denied her sleep. I have only begged her not to sleep until midday, since that involved neglecting the house and leaving the child without supervision.

JUDGE *(Interrupting)* Excuse me, Baroness. Did you lie in bed until midday?

SIRI No.

JUDGE Thank you. Proceed.

FANNY And he has left me lying ill and refused to send for a doctor.

STRINDBERG The Baroness had a habit of falling ill whenever she didn't get her own way, but that kind of illness was soon over. After having, on one occasion, called in a specialist from town, who made it clear that her illness was nothing but a sham, I summoned no doctor for her next attack—brought on, I should mention, by the fact that a new pier-glass cost fifty kronor less than the one she wanted.

PROSECUTOR None of this is of a nature that can be taken into account in determining so grave a case. There must be more serious grounds.

FANNY Surely it ought to be counted a serious ground that a father will not allow a mother to bring up her own child.

STRINDBERG *(In his role as the Baron)* In the first place, the Baroness left the care of the child to a maid, and when she herself took a hand in its supervision, things always went wrong—

JUDGE *(Interrupting)* Pardon me, but I understood you to say a moment ago that the child was without supervision when the Baroness stayed in bed until midday. Now you say it was in the charge of a maid.

(They all look at STRINDBERG *in silence. Finally, he shrugs awkwardly)*

STRINDBERG I wrote this play nearly twenty years ago. I really can't remember all the details . . .

JUDGE *(Sighing)* Very well. Proceed.

STRINDBERG In the second place, she wanted to bring up the boy to become a woman instead of a man. Thus she let him go about in girl's clothes until he was four years old, and to this day, at eight, he wears his hair long like a girl and plays with dolls. *(The* JUDGE *is about to interrupt, but thinks better of it; instead he looks interrogatively at* SIRI, *who shakes her head slowly and firmly)* At the same time, she amused herself by dressing the girls on the estate as boys . . .

PROSECUTOR And yet you are now willing to leave the child in the mother's care?

STRINDBERG Yes, I never entertained the cruel idea of separating mother and child. However, I only promised on condition that the law did not concern itself with the question. Since we have started recriminations, I have changed my mind, especially as I have ceased to be the plaintiff and become the defendant.

Colin Wilson

FANNY   That's the way this man always keeps his promises!

STRINDBERG   My promises, like other people's, are always conditional, and so long as the conditions were observed, I kept them.

FANNY   For example, he promised me personal freedom after marriage—

STRINDBERG   On the assumption, naturally, that the rules and proprieties would not be violated. But when she overstepped all bounds of decency, and freedom became another name for promiscuity, I considered my promise void.

FANNY   Yes, he constantly plagued me with the most preposterous jealousy. He was even jealous of the doctor.

STRINDBERG   This jealousy amounted to protesting against the employment of a notorious and gossiping masseur for an ailment usually treated by a woman. Unless the Baroness is referring to the occasion when I turned out the bailiff, who was smoking in the drawing room and offering her cigars—

JUDGE *(Impatiently)*   Oh, come, please! All this is simply vicious gossip. It has nothing whatever to do with literature. *(To the* PROSECUTOR*)* Does this play get anywhere?

PROSECUTOR   Not really. The Baron continues to be noble and honest, and the Baroness continues to be spiteful and

74

dishonest. At the end, her spite brings about the result she dreaded, and the child is given into the custody of two ignorant peasants, while the Baroness ends by confessing that she is evil and hysterical . . .

JUDGE *(To* STRINDBERG*)* And you still deny that this play was an act of revenge on your wife?

STRINDBERG Very well. It was an act of revenge. But I suffered for it. I have suffered constantly, all my life . . .

JUDGE And you refuse to acknowledge that this suffering has been largely your own fault?

STRINDBERG My own fault perhaps. What the prosecutor has been careful not to mention is that I have tried hard to expiate it. I've tried to rise above it to something greater. That is the meaning of my life—if it has any. It's certainly the meaning of my work. Has the prosecutor told you that in the play I wrote next I exposed my guilt to all the world?

JUDGE *(Patiently)* Herr Strindberg, I'm afraid you seem hardly aware of the gravity of the case against you. Whether you exposed your guilt or not is beside the point. You are a writer, and the custodian of certain talents. The prosecution alleges that you have completely wasted and dissipated those talents, that you have used them for purely personal ends, for spite and malice and self-glorification. Now, if this is true, it is almost the most serious charge that could be brought against you. If

I understood you rightly, you refused to make any profit on your discovery of iodine because you said that it should be for the benefit of the human race. In that case, you *do* recognize that the business of the artist is to rise above the trivial and the personal . . .

STRINDBERG *(Quietly, subdued)*   I do.

JUDGE   Can you claim that the play we have just been watching rises above the trivial and the personal? Is it not true that its attack on injustice was merely an excuse for denouncing your wife? (STRINDBERG *is silent*) Does your work ever rise above resentment and malice and wounded egoism?

STRINDBERG   My lord, I would like to ask how you can expect an artist to talk about universal meanings when he has an empty stomach?

JUDGE   Mozart and Beethoven seem to have managed it. However, we are not here to discuss that. I am asking you a simple question. You are an expert at denouncing human weakness. Do you have an understanding of human strength?

STRINDBERG *(Passionately)*   How can you judge my life in these abstract terms? All the important things about me slip through them, like fishes out of a net where the mesh is too wide. I've lived, I've suffered torments, and I've gone on writing in spite of it all. Isn't that enough?

PROSECUTOR *(Ironically)*   Torments?

STRINDBERG *(Violently)*   Yes, torments that you can't even begin to understand, that he *(Points to* STEINMETZ*)* can't understand because he's too rational and logical. Well, let me tell you this. Even if I can't justify myself to this court, it still doesn't mean I'm wrong and you're right.

(Now, as STRINDBERG *gains confidence and talks with passion, the stage around him darkens, while the light focuses on him)*

All right, you believe I went mad during my period in Paris. *(He addresses this to* STEINMETZ*)* Why do you believe I went mad? Because I began to believe there was a destiny that was punishing me for my sins. All right, well, perhaps I *did* come to believe a few things that weren't strictly true. I heard a piano playing a piece from Schumann's *Fantasie-stücke* in the next house. I used to know a Pole who was always playing it, and who had since come to hate me. I was convinced that he had come to Paris and planned to murder me. So I gathered together all my will, and willed him to die. And a few weeks later, I heard he'd been arrested in Warsaw for the murder of his mistress and baby. How do you account for that? *(Quickly, before they can reply)* Oh, don't tell me. Coincidence. Well, perhaps it was. But it couldn't *all* have been coincidence. That kind of thing happened too often. I simply had to recognize that there are unknown powers about which we know nothing. I'll give you an example. When I was ill in Paris, I suddenly had an overwhelming desire to be with my family. I wanted it so intensely that I suddenly believed that I was inside my own house. Everything was extraordinarily clear, and my mother-in-law was playing the piano. As I stood looking at her, our eyes met, and she looked startled. Well, a few days later I received a letter from her, asking me if I were ill. She said she'd been playing the piano when she suddenly saw me standing there, looking at her. She thought perhaps I'd just died. How do you account for that? Coincidence again? But do you begin to understand why it wasn't simple madness? I was in a new world. I'd lost my bearings. But it wasn't all illusion. I was catching a glimpse of some strange new powers of the human soul. Listen, I'll give you another example. One evening, I was sitting in a café talking to a young officer who had various problems and was thinking of leaving the army. I used all the arguments and appeals I could think of. Then I wanted to call up a certain past event to try and influence his resolve. I began to describe it to him: "You remember that evening in the Augustiner tavern . . ." I continued to describe the table where we had eaten our meal, the position of the bar, and so on. All of a sudden, I stopped. I had half lost consciousness, without fainting. But suddenly I was *in* the Augustiner tavern, looking at the very things I had been describing a moment before, watching strange people come in and out of the door. And yet I was still vaguely aware of also being in the café, sitting opposite the young officer. I said to him: "Listen, don't speak for a moment. I've forgotten who you are and where I am . . ." I could still see the café dimly, like a double-exposed photograph. Then, with an effort, I brought myself back to the café. And my friend suddenly burst into tears and said: "Don't ever do that again. It was terrible." He said I'd turned into a kind of living statue, as if I were alive and dead at the same time. It was experiences of this sort that convinced me that human beings possess strange powers that they normally fail to recognize. It is only in the great crises of life, when existence itself is threatened, that the soul achieves strange, transcendent powers. And so all these crises and miseries, that had almost cost me my life, had served a certain purpose after all. I suddenly became aware that the human race is on the brink of some great evolutionary leap. We all possess these powers, but the ordinary routine of life never allows us to discover them. Don't you see my point? We've come to believe that the imagination is merely a way of telling ourselves lies, of escaping reality. And yet there are two clear examples where I used my imagination to project myself to a distant place. I never bothered to check the Augustiner tavern to find out whether the people I saw had really been there at the moment I saw them. But I'm convinced they were. My experience with my mother-in-law convinces me of it, for our eyes met across the piano when I was in Paris and she was in Dornach.

Now, you see, I had been a confirmed materalist and atheist since I was fourteen. But now I began to see that the world was a more mysterious place than I'd ever realized. I began to notice all kinds of curious things, things that most people recognize but don't really think about. For example, the way that a husband and wife feel such sympathy for one another that the husband feels the wife's birth pangs. I learned this when I was married to Siri. The connection between husband and wife isn't just mutual need. It is a real bond and has palpable actuality. When I began to love Siri, I deposited my soul with her piecemeal. And I had a feeling that my love was somehow compelling her to love me, drawing her out of her neutrality, in spite of herself. Another illusion? Perhaps, yet it all fits together. When Siri left me, it actually caused a physical pain, as if she'd wrenched off my arm. All these things gave me new insights. I noticed that there are invisible threads between human beings. Go into a full railway carriage where no one knows anyone else, and everyone is silent. Everyone obviously feels a curious discomfort. It is not war, yet everyone feels as if they're stifled. It is as if threads from all their souls were crossing and tangling . . . Then someone begins to speak. A kind of electrical discharge takes place, and the various currents mingle and neutralize one another. People enter into trivial conversations out of a feeling of physical necessity. The other day I was walking along the street when I saw an innkeeper abusing a knife grinder who was standing in the gutter. As I walked between the two quarreling men, I experienced a keen feeling of discomfort, as if I'd broken a cord that was stretched tight between them, or rather, as if I'd crossed a street that was being sprinkled on both sides with water. As soon as I began to notice this, it began to happen all the time. Little coincidences, the kind that happen to everybody. You see a name that you've never heard before in your life. And within a few hours, you can bet that you'll see it at least once again. As if destiny were trying to drive home its point by repetition. Or you're feeling particularly low and miserable— and your condition seems to attract further misfortune, as a lightning conductor attracts lightning. Don't tell me, gentlemen, that for all your talk about reason and logic, you don't recognize a grain of truth in what I'm saying?

Reason and logic are all very well, but we have a deep
instinct about life. You have to live it by intuition, not by
logic. Yes, even the literary critics and the professors of
philosophy have to live by intuition.

And then, the cases in which I actually caused misfortune—or even death—by concentrating my hatred
upon a particular person. You don't have to tell *me* it
could be coincidence. I haven't forgotten the logic of
everyday life. But I'm trying to get below it, beyond it.
It doesn't go deep enough. And you have to admit that
all this fits in with what I'm saying—that perhaps man's
imagination is a more powerful instrument than he ever
realized; that perhaps he possesses power that he doesn't
know how to use. Just as a young girl possesses all the
organs for bearing children, yet can't make any use of
them until she reaches puberty. Supposing man has
reached a kind of watershed in his evolution?

This is what I came to believe through all my sufferings, during my Inferno period. No doubt I did go a
little mad. No doubt I did mistake ordinary coincidence
for the hand of fate. And yet there were other matters
that can't be explained away—absurd little matters. For
example, I was performing some experiment in the
laboratory of the Sorbonne, using a zinc bath full of acid.
When I emptied out the acid, I saw that it had made a
picture on the inside of the bath. Hills covered with
forests of firs, steep cliffs, and a castle on top of one of
the hills. Oh, I knew it was mere chance—like seeing
faces in the fire. Yet the scene was so clear that I stared
at it for a long time, imprinting it on my memory. A few
months later, I went to stay with my mother-in-law at

Dornach. And one day, out on a walk, I suddenly recognized the same scene, detail for detail—the hills, the cliffs, everything . . . Now, I'd been so impressed by the picture in the zinc bath that I'd made a sketch from it, and I was able to compare the sketch with the actual landscape. They were almost identical. So you see, I felt justified in assuming that there are hidden laws working behind human history, and my old materialism had been an excuse for mental laziness. But what hidden laws? This was a question that baffled me. I'm still not sure that I know the answer, but I think I know a part of it. It began to break on me slowly during my stay in Dornach. The answer lay in the picture in the zinc bath. You see, my mother-in-law gave me a copy of Swedenborg's *Heaven and Hell* to read. I opened it casually, without real interest—and my eye fell on a description of Hell. And again, *it was identical with the picture of the zinc bath* and with the place I was staying in! The crater-shaped valley, the wooded hills, the ravine with a stream running down it, the heaps of dung and the pigsty that I could see from my bedroom window—they were all there. (*With triumph*) What do you think of that? Madness again, eh? But I could show you my sketch of the zinc-bath landscape and show you the description in Swedenborg, and show you a photograph of the landscape at Dornach. So again you have to fall back on your talk about coincidence!

(*He prowls up and down the stage, looking at them all triumphantly. He can see that the* JUDGE *is impressed. He goes on after a moment*)

Now, I think you agree with me that if we dismiss the

idea of coincidence, then I was justified in looking for my answer in Swedenborg. Well, justified or not, that is what I did. And imagine my astonishment, my relief, my delight, in discovering that Swedenborg had described exactly my torments of the past year! They were all there, in Swedenborg's description of Hell!

Now, don't misunderstand me. I had been brought up in the profoundest contempt of the doctrine of Hell; I had consigned it to the rubbish heap of outworn ideas when I was twelve. And yet I cannot deny the fact—and this is the surprising thing about Swedenborg's doctrine of eternal punishment—that we are already in hell. Earth, this earth, is hell—the dungeon appointed by a superior power in which we can't move a step without injuring the happiness of others, in which innocence commits murder as soon as it begins to act. As soon as I read this in Swedenborg, I saw its obvious truth. And there again I recognized the destructive power of my own hatred. The old grandmother who owns the house in which I am staying has read some of my books, and hates me because of my attitude to women. She ordered her daughter to throw me out of the house, and threatened to disinherit her if she refused. So I packed my bags and prepared to go. Before I left, I shook my fist at a painting of the old woman that hung over my bed and cursed her. Two hours later, a terrible storm broke over the house. Lightning kept striking the ground, and the rain poured in torrents from a completely black sky. A week later—during which time I had stayed with another relative—the old lady became violently ill and then went insane. In one of her lucid periods, she withdrew her objection to my remaining in the valley—so I was able to move back to my mother-in-law's house. By this time, I'd got hold of another volume of Swedenborg's called *Dreams*—and this one gave me the final answer to my problems. For Swedenborg describes his own period of mental illness in 1744, and it corresponded exactly with my own. Swedenborg refers to it as "devastation," and explains that it is actually intended as a disciplinary force. Its purpose is to bring man to the threshold of a new stage in his evolution. The symptoms of devastation consist of a feeling of suffocation, heart palpitations, terrible attacks of fear, sleeplessness, nightmares, and a strange feeling as if an electric current is being driven through the chest. And all this was exactly what I'd experienced! There had been times when I had suspected that someone had concealed an electrical machine in the next room, and on one occasion I leaped out of a top-story window to escape it.

But this is not all. My own sufferings prove nothing. But when I returned to Paris, and later to Stockholm, I was always meeting acquaintances who were suffering from the same symptoms. One doctor referred to them as the "typical ailment of the twentieth century." So I do not shrink from drawing the conclusion that we are approaching a new era in which there will be a strange awakening. The whole human race is on the verge of a great change. Angina pectoris, sleeplessness, nightly terrors—what our friend here calls neurosis—are all the work of unseen powers. For how can the systematic persecution of healthy people by unprecedented bizarre occurrences be regarded as an epidemic sickness? An epidemic of coincidences! The idea is absurd!

No, the truth is that we're decadent. This civilization

is being suffocated with too much comfort. It is dying of laziness. Nietzsche was right. We're only half alive. And the fates are trying to rouse the best of us from our lethargy. It's the same principle as vaccinating someone against a disease. We're vaccinated with a small dose of madness—enough to make us fight until we're completely healthy. I tell you that human beings as they exist at the moment are a half-measure. You must admit one thing about my works—that they're full of men who aren't satisfied to be merely themselves. They want to smash and rage and tear until they've destroyed the worm of triviality that turns the heart into a rotten apple.

Oh, I've fought. Even Steinmetz admits that, don't you? The first time we met, he told me that by all rights I should have been as mad as Nietzsche. He said that I interested him because I proved that madness isn't a disease of the brain, but of the will. He said I went completely insane when I was in Paris, but luckily I never realized it. So I never ceased to struggle. I never gave in. A man's not mad until he gives in to it. Then, when the will collapses, everything collapses.

(He pauses for several seconds, waiting, as if expecting to be interrupted; then he goes on slowly)

Well, there you have it—the story of my life. I always wanted to scale the walls of heaven, but I never succeeded. Do you condemn me for that?

(There is a long pause)

JUDGE *(Suddenly clearly visible)* Have you finished?

STRINDBERG Have I said enough?

PROSECUTOR *(Impatiently)* Too much, far too much.

STRINDBERG *(Rather taken aback)* Very well, let me con-
clude by reading you something I wrote this afternoon—
the last words of what may be my last play . . . *(He takes
up papers from a table)* This is my own epitaph:

> *Here lies Ishmael, son of Hagar*
> *Who was formerly called Israel,*
> *Because his life was a battle against God,*
> *And he didn't cease to fight until exhausted,*
> *Defeat by the Eternal Benevolence.*
> *Oh Eternal One, I refuse to let go of your hand,*
> *Your stony, crushing hand, until it bless me.*
> *Bless me, your creature,*
> *Who has only suffered from your gift of life.*
> *Bless me, whose deepest suffering,*
> *Deepest of human suffering, was this:*
> *Not being the person I always wanted to be.*

*(While he has been speaking, soft music was heard
—Rachmaninov's "Island of the Dead")*

STRINDBERG There, I've finished. You can judge me now.
(The music stops. The JUDGE *utters a sigh of relief)*

JUDGE Well, you certainly have a remarkable capacity for
self-dramatization.

STRINDBERG You reject everything I say, then?

JUDGE By no means. But I'm afraid you've developed your
capacity for self-justification to such a remarkable degree

that it's difficult to sort out the sense from the nonsense. *(To the* PROSECUTOR*)* What are we going to do with him?

PROSECUTOR   There's nothing we can do. He's incorrigible.

STRINDBERG *(Proudly)*   Very well, then. Pass your sentence. *(Striding across the stage, and pausing in front of the* JUDGE*)* But remember this. You can do nothing to me that life hasn't done already.

JUDGE   Sentence? What sentence? There is no sentence.

STRINDBERG   No sentence? . . . I don't understand. Then what's the point of it?
        (He stares around the court, baffled, until the JUDGE *speaks quietly)*

JUDGE   Yes, you certainly appear to have missed the point somewhere, don't you?

STRINDBERG   Missed it? How? What do you mean? Tell me how? *(But the* JUDGE *only shrugs, and the light goes out slowly)* Stop! You can't go now. You brought me here.

JUDGE *(starting to go out)*   Did I?
        (He goes. The PROSECUTOR *also starts to go)*

STRINDBERG *(Shouting)*   If you didn't, who did? You stop! *(The* PROSECUTOR *pauses)* You can't leave me now. I want to know your verdict.

PROSECUTOR *(As he goes)* What verdict? You were only a witness.

STRINDBERG Are you trying to drive me mad? I want to know the answer—Steinmetz, you tell me.

STEINMETZ Tell you what?

STRINDBERG What did he mean . . . I'd missed the point? What point?

STEINMETZ Why have you always hated women?
(He seems to fade into the darkness)

STRINDBERG Women? Women . . . The women. *(He looks around and sees for a moment* SIRI *standing in the niche, dressed in white, as in the garden. He bursts out)* What's the good of talking about women? They all betrayed me. *(Suddenly confused as he looks at* SIRI*)* But I never hated women. I always loved them too much. *(*HARRIET *now appears on the left, dressed as earlier in the scene.* STRINDBERG *shrinks from her)* There was something about them that frightened me. *(*HARRIET *comes closer. She does not speak, but she stands in front of him as she did when asking, "Do you want me?" She reaches out to him—but the gesture is hardly more than a hint. He bends his head, closing his eyes so as not to see her, then turns away. But when he opens his eyes, he sees* INA FORSTÉN *standing near the doorway, and behind her,* FANNY. *With a kind of cry of pain)* What man doesn't want all the women in the world? They contain everything. *(He turns*

his eyes towards where STEINMETZ *was standing)* All
right, Steinmetz, I'll tell you. I've hated women because
they're a force that could destroy me. Once or twice I've
been caught in that whirlpool and . . . *(But he cannot go
on; his voice chokes)* What would have happened to me?
What would have happened? They wanted me to be a
giant, splitting the rocks apart. *(Hardly able to go on)*
But I'm not a giant. I'm a dwarf. I work underground.
That's why I turned to science—to escape from women.
My soul had to belong to me. It has to be my own, not
theirs. *(Now, leaning on the* JUDGE's *bench for support,
his face completely white, obviously undergoing some
immense inner convulsion)* Steinmetz, can you hear me?
You know about sex, don't you? *(This is an appeal)* There
are some women who can rip a man apart as an earth-
quake splits a mountain. Steinmetz. There are some
women as dangerous as an electric cable . . . Steinmetz,
don't you understand? That's what *The Father*'s about.
Woman the creator and destroyer. A woman like that can
do anything she likes with a man, because she's a magnet.
That fool Böök said the play was unreal because the husband could not leave her. But that's impossible. She's a
giant magnet, and he's only an iron nail. He can't get
away. *(Looking at* SIRI*)* I wanted to believe in woman the
virgin goddess, the poet's dream. Steinmetz, if she'd been
like that I'd have worshiped her all my life. But when I
kissed her, she put her arms around me and she let her fingers caress the back of my neck . . . long, white fingers,
very cool . . . and then I knew I'd made a mistake. I was
like a man who thinks he's bought a kitten and discovers
it's a tiger. And then she pulled me down on the floor, in

the middle of all the papers. Or was that another time? I can't remember . . . All I can remember is that sensation of touching an electric cable . . . (*He looks at* SIRI *again and falters, confused*) I don't seem to understand anything any more . . . Was I wrong? (*He stares intently at her, and memories return*) The virgin goddess. That night on the steamer . . . (*He turns away, closing his eyes*) But she betrayed me. They all betrayed me. (*He stares intently towards* STEINMETZ, *who is only dimly visible behind the* JUDGE's *chair*) How *could* I have been wrong? How can a thing possess opposite qualities at the same time? It must have been an illusion . . .

SIRI (*Quietly*)   Was it?
        (*He starts and looks around. She has left the niche and stands close behind him—yet still oddly unreal*)

STRINDBERG (*Looking at her, then at* HARRIET *and* FANNY) Don't. I can't stand any more. If I'm going to die, let me die. But don't ask me to live it over again.
        (*He sits, and buries his face in his hands*)

SIRI (*With genuine compassion*)   You don't even begin to understand, do you?
        (*He looks up at her, wanting to understand but afraid*)

STRINDBERG   Understand what?

SIRI   Do you know why I married Gustav? Because he wasn't like the other officers. He seemed finer, nobler.

90

Oh, I knew he drank and told indecent stories with the others, but it wasn't his true nature. *(Now he begins to understand, and his eyes become haunted and strained)* I married him because I thought he was a poet. *(He starts as if she had struck him)* It's something every woman wants to do, even if she wouldn't admit it. *(She turns away from him, speaking softly, half to herself)* She knows she possesses a power over certain men, power to turn them into poets. And, in doing it, she escapes her own limitations. She learns to use his eyes, to see herself as he sees her. *(She now looks at* STRINDBERG *with candid eyes)* Through his eyes, she sees herself as a virgin goddess. *(He shudders and looks away)* When I married Gustav that's what happened for the first few months. *(She now goes away to the other side of the stage, as if she wanted to lessen the impact of what she is about to say)* But he couldn't live up to the vision. He was a good man. He had a fine nature. But he was weak. He found life more comfortable in the officers' mess. I didn't blame him. I blamed myself for failing him, for being a dissatisfied romantic, for reading novels when I could have been gossiping with the other officers' wives. That's why I didn't blame him even when he started to be unfaithful. His cousin was the sort of woman he should have married. She wouldn't have made him dream. But Gustav didn't really have the strength to dream . . .

(She goes back and stands behind STRINDBERG*)*

Then you came along, and I knew you were stronger than Gustav. It seemed obvious we were made for each other—you the poet, I the romantic who couldn't be contented with anything less. *(Silence)* So why did it fail?

STRINDBERG *(Afraid to look at her)* Because you betrayed me.

SIRI Did I? I was never unfaithful. I loved you. I wanted to bear your children and run your home. But I had no power to be anything more than a housewife. Only you could give me that power—as you gave it to me that night on the steamer. Don't you understand? If I was to see myself as anything more than a housewife, it had to be through your eyes. You never seemed to understand your own strength. You never believed in it. So what could I do? When I looked into your eyes I saw nothing but defeat and mistrust. At first I blamed myself. I blamed myself even after we'd separated and you wrote that unfair book. But then I read the book you wrote about your second marriage, and I saw that it had nothing to do with me. *(Silence for a moment, then she says very explicitly)* You wanted a goddess, but you were afraid to be a god.

STRINDBERG Is it possible to be a god?

SIRI *(Smiling ruefully)* How do I know? I'm only a woman. But I was willing to believe in you.

STRINDBERG *(Standing up, suddenly almost calm)* They all were . . . They all were. *(Tiredly)* But I'm not a god. I'm a dwarf, a pygmy—as she called me. *(Pointing to HARRIET)* I don't know why I failed. Is there a reason? Is there ever a reason? I suppose that's what freedom means. You can't choose when to succeed. But you can choose when to surrender . . . I don't know how far the others

were to blame—my mother, my father, my wives, and all
the mean and envious busybodies . . .

(Suddenly, with an immense effort)

I know. I'm doing it again. But what does it matter?
It's too late now anyway. He was right. This isn't a trial.
It's an inquest. An inquest on a corpse called Johann
Augustus Strindberg. *(He points to the figure in the bed
in the corner)* He should have found himself out twenty
years ago, while there was still time . . .

HARRIET *(Suddenly speaking sharply)* Is it too late?

STRINDBERG   Oh, yes, it's too late. *(He presses his hands
to his stomach)* I've a pain here, a dull sort of pain. Do
you know what it is? It's my life smoldering itself out.
That's why there was no trial. I'd already tried myself.
And sentenced myself to death. That's the logical conclusion of a lifelong defeat. *(The light is becoming so dim
that only* STRINDBERG *is now visible. But he makes an
effort, as if unwilling to be consigned to the night)* But
is there another way? *(The light strengthens, focused on
him, as he asks with sudden strength)* If so, what is it?
There must be another way, if life's not to end in death,
in a mockery of everything we stand for. There's an invisible will to death, and man has to be saved from it.
I've put it into my last play, into *The Great Highway.*
It's symbolized by a Japanese called Hiroshima. He wants
to purify himself—to purify his flesh as well as his soul.
So he makes a will ordering that his body should be
cremated, and then takes a sleeping draught that makes
him appear to be dead . . .

(He laughs) I must have been insane when I wrote it. That kind of fire doesn't purify. It only destroys. But how did this hidden will to death creep into man's heart? How did it creep into my stomach?

What if it creeps into the stomach of the world? What if all the world ends in flames like Hiroshima? *(Almost frenziedly)* It has got to be torn out, this will to death. *(He claws at his own stomach)* Somehow . . . it's got to be torn out. I should have understood sooner . . .

(There is a muffled cry—but it comes from the bed, where STRINDBERG *is asleep. The stage is suddenly completely black, with only a light burning near the bed.* STRINDBERG *stirs uneasily in his sleep and half sits up. The figure of* SIRI *appears for a moment, dressed in white. Then vanishes in darkness.)*

Curtain

About the Author

Colin Wilson's brilliant first book, *The Outsider,* gained him an international reputation. He has since written almost thirty books in genres as varied as science fiction, detective and spy stories; penetrating psychological studies; scholarly works and a number of novels. He lives in England with his wife and two children.